SCHOLASTIC

Reteaching Math

DATA ANALYSIS & PROBABILITY

Mini-Lessons, Games & Activities to Review
& Reinforce Essential Math Concepts & Skills

Maryann McMahon-Nester & Bob Krech

New York • Toronto • London • Auckland • Sydney
Mexico City • New Delhi • Hong Kong • Buenos Aires

Teaching *Resources*

DEDICATION

For Quentin, Alex, Brandon, and Andrew.
Thanks for the support.
—MMN

ACKNOWLEDGMENTS

Sincere thanks to Bob Krech for giving me this opportunity.
—MMN

Many thanks to our patient editors, Maria Chang and Mela Ottaiano!
—BK

Editor: Mela Ottaiano
Cover design by Brian LaRossa
Interior design by Holly Grundon
Interior illustrations by Mike Moran

ISBN-13: 978-0-439-52965-5
ISBN-10: 0-439-52965-4

Table of Contents

Table of Contents (continued)

Introduction

Most math books that have the word *reteaching* in the title typically feature many pages of equations and practice problems. The reasoning may be that if students require a concept or skill to be retaught, the best way for them to gain mastery is to practice more of the same. Research does show that some students need more time on a task than other students in order to learn a concept. However, if a student does not understand a concept or skill the first time, presenting a series of problems that the student already finds difficult and repeating them, without new knowledge or intervention, will most likely not be successful.

To reteach implies actually teaching again, not merely repeated practice. Students need to have a strong conceptual understanding if they are going to be able to do mathematics with accuracy and comprehension. Without this understanding, math can become meaningless and students simply work by rote. That's why we've created the Reteaching Math series. You will find this series is different from most reteaching books in that the emphasis is on helping students develop understanding as well as providing useful practice.

Using a Problem-Solving Approach

The activities, games, and lessons in this book are just plain good instruction, with an emphasis on solving problems and applying math in context. Problem solving is the first process standard listed in the NCTM *Principles and Standards for School Mathematics* (2000). The accompanying statement reads, "Problem solving should be the central focus of all mathematics instruction and an integral part of all mathematical activity." In other words, problem solving is what math is all about. Every lesson here begins with a problem to solve to help create a spirit of inquiry and interest. Practice problems are integrated into the lessons so they are meaningful. Real reteaching!

Providing Context

It is important to provide students with a context to help give learning mathematical skills and concepts meaning. Context helps learners understand how these mathematical ideas and tools are useful and can be applied to real-life problems and situations. Context can be provided by creating a theme that carries throughout all the lessons. In this book, the theme of The 13th Annual Dataville County Games Fair provides a context in which learning about data and probability is relevant, motivating, and fun. A generous dose of humor is included to help ease the anxiety many students feel over data analysis and probability in particular, and math in general. The use of the overarching games theme gives all the lessons a sense of cohesion, purpose, and interest.

What's Inside?

Activity Lessons – introduce major concepts and skills. Timed to last about 40 minutes, these lessons are designed to help students work on the ideas in a hands-on manner and context to help them understand the meaning behind the math and give them an opportunity to apply it in a fun way.

Practice Pages – specially designed to provide both practice and a helpful reference sheet for students. Each practice page begins with a word problem so students can see how and why the math is useful in solving real problems. Each page also features a **Basics Box**. Here, concepts are carefully presented with words, numbers, pictures, definitions, and step-by-step explanations. **Example problems** help solidify understanding, then a series of problems give students practice. Finally, a **journal prompt** helps students discuss and explore the concept using pictures, numbers, and words, while providing you an assessment opportunity that looks at student thinking and understanding. Practice pages can be worked on together in class, assigned to be done independently, or given as homework assignments.

Review Pages – provide students with additional focused practice on a specific math concept. The concept is practiced in a variety of formats and is designed to be completed independently. In addition, a mixed review of concepts introduced earlier is included in many review pages. By spiraling the curriculum in this way, students' retention and recall of math ideas is supported. These pages may be used for review, practice, homework, or assessment of students' knowledge and understanding.

Addressing Various Learning Styles

A good way to help all students learn mathematics well is to present ideas through physical, pictorial, and symbolic representations. Research suggests the importance of learning math ideas through modeling with manipulatives. Math concepts need to be experienced on a physical level before pictorial and more abstract representations can be truly understood. Relying completely on symbolic representations (e.g., lots of equations) is rarely enough, particularly in a reteaching situation.

Learning experiences featured here include using manipulatives, drawing pictures, writing equations, reading stories, and playing games to help learners gain a strong conceptual knowledge.

About Data and Probability

Data is defined as factual information, especially information organized for analysis or used to reason or make decisions. Probability can be defined as the chance or likelihood of a certain outcome. Data analysis and probability are important concepts that are gaining increased focus in the elementary school classroom. Students need to be able to interpret data in their everyday lives. With sufficient exposure starting in the elementary classroom, students will be able to use data analysis and probability to better understand the world around them and make informed decisions.

How to Use This Book

This book can be used as a replacement unit, as a resource for activities for math workshops or centers, or as a supplement to find engaging ideas to enhance a textbook unit. The lessons and activities are presented in a developmental sequence, but can be used as stand-alone or supplementary learning experiences. Since it's written to accommodate all learners, you can use it to teach a unit on data and probability to any class.

Data and probability are discussed in the NCTM Standards under the Data Analysis and Probability Standard. The expectations include:

- formulate questions that can be addressed with data; and collect, organize, and display relevant data to answer them

- select and use appropriate statistical methods to analyze data

- develop and evaluate inferences and predictions that are based on data

- understand and apply basic concepts of probability

Within these expectations are more specific objectives for grades 2–4. These are addressed in the learning experiences throughout this book and include:

- classify objects by attributes

- interpret and analyze data based on bar graphs, pictographs, tables, Venn diagrams, line graphs, line plots, circle graphs, lists, and tree diagrams

- collect, analyze, and display data in an organized way using and/or constructing bar graphs, pictographs, tables, Venn diagrams, line graphs, line plots, circle graphs, lists, and tree diagrams

- introduce and discuss median, mode, range, and outliers

- find and/or calculate median, mode, and range

- generate and organize data using spinners, number cubes, and dice

- discuss the probability of events using terms such as most often, least often, fair, unfair, possible, impossible, likely, unlikely, and certain

Whatever the concept, students maintain interest and gain a better understanding when the problems are meaningful to them. When studying data analysis and probability, students should be involved firsthand in the collection of data and activities that lead to the collection of data. The same holds true for hands-on activities that foster your students' understanding of probability.

Part 1: Collecting and Analyzing Data

Materials

For each student:
- Practice Page #1 (p. 29)
- Review Page #1 (p. 30)
- pencil

For each group of 4–6 students:
- What is your favorite ____? (p. 27)
- What I Have Learned From the Data (p. 28)

For teacher:
- one piece each of green, orange, blue, and yellow construction paper
- Transparency of What is your favorite ____?
- overhead markers

Teaching Tip

Data/Probability Word Wall

A lot of vocabulary will emerge in this unit. Record it on a word wall bulletin board or large chart. Write the words clearly. Include examples and pictures or diagrams. Student pairs can draw and label certain terms for the chart. This classroom reference can continually be expanded. As words are added, have students add them to a chart of their own in their math journals. Continually add new vocabulary as it appears in the lessons.

Data, Data Everywhere

(COLLECTING DATA WITH SURVEYS)

> Objective: Students will survey the class and collect data about "favorites."

Say, "Today, we are going to find out about some of the 'favorites' in our class. What does 'favorite' mean? *(liked best of all or preferred over the rest)* Pretend that we are going to paint our classroom walls. We have four colors of paint to choose from: blue, yellow, green, or orange." Show a piece of construction paper for each color.

Continue, "I want you to choose the one color that would be your favorite for our walls. Please close your eyes. Raise your hand when I say the color that you choose. I will count how many hands go up and write that number on the colored paper." Do this for the four colors. Leave the results displayed and discuss.

Ask, "What did we find out?" Allow students to *analyze* and respond. If needed, ask questions such as, "Which color did most people choose? Which color was chosen the least? How do you know?"

Say, "That was a short survey that gave us some data. What do you think I mean by 'survey'? *(a process where a group of people are asked the same question)* Surveys give us data. What is data?" *(information, especially numerical information)*

Explain, "Today you are going to get into groups (of 4–6) and do a survey that will provide us with some interesting data about our class." Hold up a copy or on the overhead show a copy of the What is your favorite ____? sheet (p. 27).

Continue, "In your group you will decide on a question about a favorite to ask the class. For example, you might complete this form by writing 'What is your favorite <u>pet</u>?' You can see the spaces to write your names and four spaces for choices. You have to give your survey-takers choices. For pets, we might write cats, dogs, birds, and hamsters. We can't list all the possibilities so try to pick what you feel would be the most popular. In the Directions space you need to write down how people will show their choices, such as with a tally mark or check mark or smiley face." Do this particular survey question on the overhead or board with your class as an example.

Put the students into groups and assign a recorder for each group. Each group gets one What is your favorite ____? sheet. Allow students a few minutes to prepare their surveys. When they are finished, have a member of each group briefly explain his or her group's survey and directions to the class. Put the surveys on different desks in the classroom and allow each student to mark each survey. When this is completed, have the groups get back together and analyze the data from the survey they prepared. Each student should complete the What I Have Learned From the Data sheet (p. 28). Groups can present their analysis of the data to the class the following day.

End this lesson with a brief explanation of *analysis*. Say, "During this lesson, we gathered data on some 'favorites.' We talked about what we learned. When we look at data to see what we can learn, we call it analyzing the data." Once the class has come up with an accurate and meaningful definition of *analysis*, add it to the word wall.

Teaching Tip

Special Delivery

Many of the activities in this unit are in the form of a letter from Bruce B. Fairplay, Dataville Games Chairman. It adds to the excitement and interest if each new lesson letter/material arrives in a mailing envelope addressed to the class. Include enough copies in the envelope for all of the students to work individually or in small groups.

ACTIVITY LESSON #2

The 13th Annual Dataville County Games Fair

(PICTOGRAPHS AND BAR GRAPHS)

Objective: Students will read and make simple bar graphs and pictographs based on a table of data.

Materials

For each student:
- Letter #2 (p. 31)
- Table of Sports Competition Participation (p. 32)
- Pictograph and Pictograph Pieces (pp. 33 and 34)
- Bar Graph (p. 35)
- pencil, scissors, glue stick
- Practice Page #2 (pp. 36 and 37)
- Review Page #2 (p. 38)

Begin this lesson by reviewing the terms *data* and *analysis*. Refer to the class word wall for definitions and examples. Say, "This is a great time for us to learn about data analysis because we have been asked to help manage the data for the 13th Annual Dataville County Games Fair. Each year Dataville County invites all of the local towns to participate in a week of friendly competitions and games of chance. According to this letter I have received, it will be our job to collect, record, organize, and analyze all kinds of data for the fair."

Pass out a copy of the letter (p. 31) to each student. Give students an opportunity to read silently and then take turns reading it aloud

Literature Links

. . . .

The Best Vacation Ever
by Stuart J. Murphy
(HarperCollins, 1997)

In rhyming prose we learn about a young girl's busy family. They all need a vacation but can't decide where to go. To help with this dilemma the girl takes a survey and then charts the results of the family preferences. The results are tallied and a decision is made about the best vacation spot, based on the data. This is an easy-to-read picture book that demonstrates the basic ideas behind posing a question, taking a survey, organizing data, and interpreting data.

Lemonade for Sale
by Stuart J. Murphy
(HarperCollins, 1998)

In this interesting picture book from the Mathstart series, three children and their parrot run a lemonade stand and keep track of their sales data with bar graphs. This is a good illustration of how representing data with graphs can make relationships and ideas more visible and understandable.

together. Ask the class, "What are we being asked to do?" (*Organize data from a table onto graphs*)

Say, "Let's take a look at that data Mr. Fairplay mentioned." Pass out copies of the Table of Sports Competition Participation (p. 32), Pictograph (p. 33), Pictograph Pieces (p. 34), and Bar Graph (p. 35).

Hold up a copy of the Table and say, "We have been asked to organize the information, or data, from this table onto graphs. Who can explain what a graph is?" (*A graph is information that is represented in the form of a picture, diagram, or drawing*)

Say, "Mr. Fairplay is asking you to create two different kinds of graphs; a pictograph and a bar graph. If I wanted to graph the number of boys and girls in this class I could use a pictograph. A pictograph uses simple pictures to represent data." (Do a count of boys and girls and represent these numbers with a simple pictograph on the board.)

Continue, "I could take this same information and display it on a bar graph." Draw a simple bar graph on the board. Say, "Each graph gives us the same information, but in different forms. Pictographs show it with pictures. Bar graphs show it with bars. People who are interested in the information can just glance at the graphs and get some information about our class. It would take them longer to read this same information if it was written out in sentences on a report."

Tell students, "You have the materials to create a bar graph and a pictograph of Mr. Fairplay's data. Please work with a partner to do that now. When you are done making your graphs, be sure to answer the sports participation questions at the bottom of your bar graph." When this work is completed, review finished graphs and answers to the question sheet together.

Activity: Graphing Bulletin Board

As a homework assignment or in-class research project, ask students to bring in examples of bar graphs and pictographs from newspapers, magazines, and the Internet. Have them identify the type of graph and write two statements about information that they learned from reading the graph. Try to provide some examples of bar graphs and pictographs that are both vertical and horizontal. Students tend to think a bar graph can only be created in a vertical format and that pictographs should be horizontal. Seeing examples of a variety of graphs helps widen their notions of the possibilities. As you continue to explore data representation, you can change or add new graphs, such as pie charts and Venn diagrams, to your display.

ACTIVITY LESSON #3

Lay It on the Line

(LINE PLOTS AND RANGE)

Objective: Students will read, analyze, and create line plots and analyze while answering questions about the data represented. The concept of range of data is also introduced.

Tell the class, "Another letter has arrived from Mr. Fairplay!" Pass out a copy of the letter (p. 39) to each student. Allow them time to read silently, then read together aloud. Say, "Aha! They have sent us a line plot. Do you know what that is? Let's look at it." Hold up a copy or look at the overhead copy of p. 40 together.

Say, "A line plot is a way of organizing data. It is a type of graph that uses a horizontal number line. A mark is made above the numbers on the line to show a result with that value. For example, on this first line plot here, we see bowling scores for the team from Brook Point. You see the score of 142 on the line? Above it are two dots. That means two bowlers from the Brook Point team each got that same score. If you look at the Marshtown bowlers, you'll see they have one dot above the number 147. That means they have one bowler who made that score. How many bowlers from Brook Point scored a 147?" (one) So each dot indicates the score of one bowler."

Explain, "Notice that these line plots don't start at zero. They don't have to. You can start and end line plots wherever it makes sense to. Since nobody scored lower than 140 or higher than 162 that's where these line plots begin and end." Ask, "Why do you think some numbers have no dots above them?" (No bowler got that score.)

Say, "I see in his letter that Mr. Fairplay is asking us to analyze the line plots and answer some questions in a table of data. He is also asking us to combine these line plots into one larger line plot and to answer questions about that as well. Let's get started." Pass out copies of Bowling Competition Results (p. 40), Bowling Competition Results Analysis (p. 41), Combined Bowling Results (p. 42), long strips of paper, rulers, and pencils. You may want to do one or two of the early examples together to model transferring data from the line plots to the table. (Note: This task can be assigned to small groups or individuals. Distribute materials accordingly.)

After students have worked for a while they will encounter the question about range. Stop at that point and explain, "Range may be a new idea for us here. Range is the difference between the lowest

Materials

For each student:
- Letter #3 (p. 39)
- Bowling Competition Results line plots (p. 40)
- Bowling Competition Results Analysis (p. 41)
- Combined Bowling Results (p. 42)
- pencil
- long strips of white drawing paper (approx. 14–16" x 4")
- Practice Page #3 (p. 43)
- Review Page #3 (p. 44)

For teacher:
- Transparency of Bowling Competition Results line plots
- overhead markers

Literature Link

....

Tiger Math: Learning to Graph From a Baby Tiger by Ann Whitehead Nagda and Cindy Bickel (Henry Holt, 2000)

T. J. is a Siberian tiger cub at the Denver Zoo. This book follows T. J. as he grows, using photographs and a variety of graphs to chart his age and weight. Very good examples of pictographs, bar graphs, and line graphs are shown in an engaging context.

Materials

....

For each student:

- History of High and Low Bowling Scores (p. 45)
- journal
- pencil
- calculator (optional)
- Practice Page #4 (p. 46)
- Review Page #4 (p. 47)

and highest results in a set of data. (*In this case, bowling scores.*) If we have three bowling scores and they are 142, 145, and 149, the range is seven, which is the difference between the lowest and highest score. Some mathematicians describe this range as being 'from 142 to 149.' This is another way to talk about range."

Allow students to share their understanding of ways to find the difference between two numbers. (*Students may choose to use subtraction or they may choose to "count up." Remind students who count up not to count the number they start on.*)

As students work and create the combined line plot, discuss with them which number can be the first one on the line plot and which can be the last. Remind them again that all numbers between the first and last number must be included. Have students use longer strips of paper to allow for enough room to neatly arrange all needed numbers on the line plot. After completing the combined line plot, check to see that students answer the questions on p. 42. Review these results together.

....

ACTIVITY LESSON #4

Some Mean Bowling

(Mean, Median, and Mode)

> Objective: Students learn how to analyze a set of data by identifying the *mean, mode,* and *median*.

B egin this lesson by referring back to the last lesson on calculating range. Say, "Think about the bowling scores sent to us by Mr. Fairplay. One of the things we did when we analyzed the scores was to find the range. Who can remind us what range is?" (*The difference between the lowest and highest number in a series of numbers.*) Ask, "How else might we analyze these bowling scores?" (*Give students a chance to make responses.*)

Tell the class, "Today we are going to look at three other common ways to analyze a series of numbers like the bowling scores." Write the following series of numbers on the board: 16, 12, 15, 12, 12, 18, 17, 12, 21 and have students copy them into their journals. Ask, "What do you notice about these numbers?" (*Responses should include things such* as, *"There are nine numbers. There are 4 twelves. The lowest number is 12. The highest number is 21. The numbers are not in order."*)

Say, "One of the ways to analyze this data is to find the *mean*. The mean is another way to say the *average*. The average is found by adding all of the numbers together and then dividing by the amount of numbers that were added." Demonstrate this on the board with the numbers above. Say, "If we add these together we get 135. We then divide this by the number of scores, which is 9, and the answer is 15. So 15 is the mean or average score."

Say, "Another way to analyze this data is to find the median score. The median is the number that is exactly in the middle of the series of numbers. To find that, we rewrite them in order from the lowest to the highest number. If a number is repeated, like the number 12 is, include it as many times as in the original series." Have a student write the ordered numbers on the board. Say, "Now that we have the numbers in order, I would like you to find the median. The median is the number in the middle." *(The students should identify 15 as the median.)*

Say, "The next way to analyze this data is to identify the mode. The mode is the number that occurs most often in a series of numbers. Which number has occurred most often in the series of numbers we have been looking at?" *(The students should identify the number 12.)* Continue, "Now that we have identified the mean, mode, and median, who can tell me what the range is for this set of numbers?" *(The range is 9, because 21 – 12 = 9.)*

Hand out the History of High and Low Bowling Scores sheet. Tell the students, "Along with the bowling score line plots for this year's games, Mr. Fairplay included the team with the highest scores and the team with the lowest scores during the entire history of the Dataville County Games. Please pair up and work together to analyze this data, finding the range, mean, mode, and median." Calculators can be used during this process. When completed, review these answers together on the board.

Materials

For each student:

- Letter #5 (p. 48)
- 2-Circle Venn Diagram (p. 49)
- 3-Circle Venn Diagram (p. 50)
- Table of Sports Competition Participation (p. 32)
- pencil
- Practice Page #5 (p. 51)
- Review Page #5 (p. 52)

Teaching Tip

Getting Physical With Venn Diagrams

You can have students create Venn diagrams on a more concrete level by the use of hula hoops or rope. Overlap hula hoops or rope to form Venn diagram circles on the floor. Supply students with manipulatives such as multilink cubes, pattern blocks, keys, or even playing cards. Have a group of students sort these items into the Venn diagram. Then have the rest of the class try to figure out the sorting rule.

ACTIVITY LESSON #5

When to Use a Venn Diagram

(Venn Diagrams)

Objective: Students will organize data on Venn diagrams and analyze the data to answer questions.

Begin by asking, "Do any of you have a brother or sister?" As hands go up and you take answers, stop after three or four and say, "That is so much information. Let's see if we can organize it a little better."

Draw two large circles on the board. Have a section of one circle overlap the other. Label one circle "sister," the other "brother," and the overlapping space "both." Say, "This is a special kind of drawing called a Venn diagram. It's used to organize data, particularly where we have some data that might fit into more than one category. I'll show you what I mean. This diagram will organize information about you and whether you have a brother or a sister or both. I'll call you up three at a time. When you come up, write your name in this circle if you have a sister or sisters, this circle if you have a brother or brothers, and in this shared part of both circles if you have both. If you don't have any brothers or sisters, write your name outside of the circles."

After everyone has written their name, ask what can be said about the class from looking at the data. *(How many students have brothers, how many have sisters, how many have both, how many have neither)*

Say, "We did a little practice with a Venn diagram because I noticed in our new letter from Mr. Fairplay that he wants us to use one. Let's read and find out about it." Pass out a copy of the letter (p. 48) to each student. Read silently, then take turns reading aloud.

Continue, "I see Mr. Fairplay wants quite a few Venn diagrams. We will break into groups to complete these." Assign students in groups of two or three to each Venn diagram requested in the letter. As students use the table (p. 32) to complete the diagrams, post them on the board for everyone to see. In addition to a two-circle Venn, each group should also complete a three-circle Venn.

ACTIVITY LESSON #6

A Piece of the Pie

(PIE CHARTS)

> Objective: In this lesson, student will analyze data on a pie chart.

Materials

For each student:
- Letter #6 (p. 53)
- Dataville Annual Pie Contest Entries Pie Chart and Questions (p. 54)
- colored pencils
- Practice Page #6 (pp. 55 and 56)
- Review Page #6 (p. 57)

Tell the class, "Guess what? We have another letter from Dataville, and this letter is accompanied by a pie chart . . . about pie!" Pass out a copy of the letter (p. 53) and the pie chart with the questions (p. 54) to each student. Read silently, then aloud together.

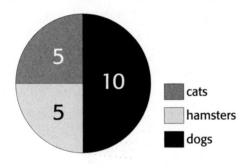

cats
hamsters
dogs

Say, "Let's take a look at what they mean by a pie chart. A pie chart is also called a circle graph." Draw a circle on the board. Continue, "It's a way to organize data and compare parts of a whole easily. For example, let's say this pie chart is about 20 pets we saw at a store: 10 of them were dogs, 5 were cats, and 5 were hamsters. To show that on this pie chart we would draw a line down the middle to split the circle in half. We would write a 10 on one half and shade it to represent dogs, because half of 20 is 10. Notice that it's important to have a key to show what the shading or color represents." Make a key that shows the shading or colors for the three different animal types.

Continue representing this example data on the pie chart. Tell students, "You can see why it is called a pie chart. It is round like a pie, and has pieces." Ask, "What do you notice about the pieces of the pie? Why is this? *(They are different sizes. Different sizes represent different amounts, in this case, different amounts of pets.)* Say, "So the pie is the whole set of animals, and the pieces represent the different amounts of animal types."

Explain, "Now if we look at the pie chart from Dataville, we can see there is a key with some different flavor pies. Use the pie chart to answer the questions on the sheet." After students complete this work, review answers together.

Materials

For each student:
- Dataville Annual Pie Contest Entries Pie Chart (p. 54)
- Fortieths Circle (p. 58)
- 5 crayons; orange, green, red, purple, and yellow
- Practice Page #7 (p. 59)
- Review Page #7 (p. 60)
- pencil

Literature Link

Gator Pie by Louise Mathews (Dodd, Mead 1979)

Alvin and Alice, two young alligators, find a pie. They decide to cut it in half and share it, but before they can, another alligator stomps up and demands a piece. More visitors arrive and Alvin and Alice continue to calculate fractions (pieces) to try to accommodate everyone. This book makes a nice connection to looking at fractions in the context of a pie chart.

ACTIVITY LESSON #7

A Fraction of a Pie
(PIE CHART FRACTIONS)

Objective: Students will learn about representing sections of a pie chart using fractions. (Note: Some previous basic fraction knowledge is assumed here.)

Draw three (same-sized) circles on the board. Divide one circle into fourths, one into sixths, and one into eighths. Ask, "What do you notice about what I drew on the board?" (*Observations might include: Each is a circle. One circle is cut into four pieces. One is cut into six pieces. One is cut into eight pieces. All of the pieces in each circle are the same size. The circles are the same size. The more pieces you have, the smaller the pieces are.*)

Shade in one section of the first circle (one of four sections). Ask, "What did I do to this first circle?" (*Shaded in one piece or section*) Ask, "How much of this circle is shaded?" (*Responses might include one out of four or one fourth.*) Ask, "When we say one fourth of something, what are we using to describe the size?" (*Fractions*) Now shade 2 pieces of the circle cut into six pieces. Ask, "How much of this circle did I shade?" (*Two out of six pieces or two sixths*) Repeat this again by shading in 6 of the 8 pieces and asking how much of the circle is shaded. Say, "Now let's look at the three circles on the board. We know all three circles are the same size. But each of the circles has a different amount shaded. And each shaded area is represented by a different fraction. Why is this so?" (*Because the fraction that is shaded comes from how many pieces are shaded out of how many equal pieces make up the whole circle.*)

Give each student a copy of the pie chart from Lesson #6 (p. 54). Ask, "How is this pie chart like the fraction circles on the board?" (*They are all circles. They are all cut into pieces.*) "How are they different?" (*The pieces are different sizes and there are numbers labeling each piece.*) "What do the numbers represent?" (*How many of each type of pie was entered into the contest.*) "How did we find the total amount of pies entered into the contest?" (*By adding all of the numbers.*) "How many pies were entered?" (*40*)

Hand out a copy of the Fortieths Circle (p. 58). Tell students, "Starting at the top of the circle and moving clockwise, color the first 15 pieces of the circle orange. Color the next 10 green. Color the next 4 red, the next 6 purple, and the last 5 yellow."

When they are finished coloring, ask them to compare their colored circle to the Dataville Pie Chart.

Say, "Sometimes when we look at a pie chart we can get an even more exact idea about how big certain sections are in relation to other sections by talking about the sections in terms of fractions. Fractions are another way we can communicate about data and probability." Ask, "Who can tell me what fraction of your colored circle is orange?" (15/40) "What does fifteen-fortieths mean?" (*Fifteen out of forty pieces.*)

Have students partner up and identify the fractions for the rest of the sections of the pie chart. If the class has already studied fractions, you may wish to see if any of the fractions can be reduced. Review these answers together.

ACTIVITY LESSON #8

The Ups and Downs of Line Graphs
(*LINE GRAPHS*)

Objective: Students learn how to read and make line graphs while observing trends that may be indicated by the data.

Announce to students, "Another letter from Dataville has arrived." Pass out a copy of the letter (p. 61) and the line graph (p. 62) to each student. Allow students time to read the letter silently, then read aloud together. Say, "In this letter, Mr. Fairplay mentions the word 'trend.' What do you think that means?" Discuss answers. (*A trend is the general tendency or direction in which something moves.*) Arrive at a definition together and add to your word wall.

Say, "Now we have a line graph here. Let's take a look at it." Show the line graph on the overhead as students follow on their own copies. Ask, "What is this a graph of?" (*The first five years of attendance at the Games.*) Say, "We usually find this information in the title, and all graphs should have a title."

Ask, "What do you think those numbers on the left side of the graph mean?" (*The number of people who attended.*) Ask, "How are these numbers organized?" (*By hundreds.*) Say, "This side of the graph is called the y axis."

Ask, "What do the numbers on the bottom section of the graph mean?" (*The years this information was collected.*) Say, "This side of the

Materials

For each student:
- Letter #8 (p. 61)
- Dataville Annual Games Fair Attendance line graph (p. 62)
- Teams Participating Data/Line Graph (p. 63)
- Pie Entries Data/Line Graph (p. 64)
- Bowling Average Data/Line Graph (p. 65)
- Practice Page #8 (p. 66)
- Review Page #8 (p. 67)
- pencil

For teacher:
- Transparency of Dataville Annual Games Fair Attendance line graph
- overhead markers

graph is called the x axis. Also, it's important to know that line graphs usually tell us about events that take place over time, and here we see that with the listing of the years."

Ask, "If we look at the line marked 'Year 1' we see a dot on that line at the horizontal line marked '300.' What does that mean?" (*It means that 300 people attended the fair in Year 1.*) Work through another example with students if necessary, or if students are ready, have them work in pairs to answer the questions on the graph. Then review the answers together as a class.

Say, "Now you should begin to create the line graphs requested by Mr. Playfair." Pass out a copy of the data and line graph templates for Teams Participating (p. 63), Pie Entries (p. 64), and Bowling Average (p. 65) to each student. Students can do all three individually or you can assign different students to different graphs or set up groups or partnerships.

When these are completed (probably the next class period) review together. As students work, pay particular attention to what kind of numbering system they choose for the y axis. This can lead to some valuable discussion.

Materials

For each student:

- Letter #9 (p. 68)
- Combos Tree Diagram (p. 69)
- Combos Table (p. 70)
- pencils
- Practice Page #9 (p. 71)
- Review Page #9 (p. 72)

ACTIVITY LESSON #9

The Quick Stop Snack Shack

(*TREE DIAGRAMS AND COMBINATIONS*)

> Objective: Students use a tree diagram to show combinations.

Tell students, "We have another letter from Mr. Fairplay and this time it's about food." Pass out a copy of the letter (p. 68) to each student. Allow time to read silently and then read aloud together. Say, "Mr. Fairplay mentions a 'tree diagram' in the letter. A tree diagram is another way to organize information or data. It's particularly helpful when you are trying to find out how many combinations are possible in a situation. Let me show you with an example."

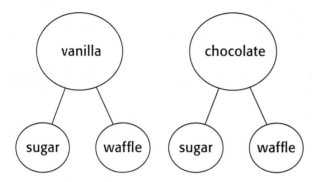

Literature Link

....

A Three Hat Day
by Laura Geringer
(Harper and Row, 1985)

R. R. Pottle III's father collected canes, and his mother collected umbrellas. He collects hats and selects his hats each day before he even gets out of bed. Throughout the story, Mr. Pottle wears his hats in combinations, sometimes two or three at a time. This story provides lots of material for a discussion of combinations of clothing and outfits.

Say, "There was an ice cream shop that only sold two flavors of ice cream: chocolate and vanilla. They also sold two kinds of cones: sugar cone and waffle cone. If we were asked to find all of the combinations of ice cream and cones, we could show it easily with a tree diagram."

Draw two large circles and write "vanilla" in one and "chocolate" in the other. Draw two branches off of each circle. At the bottom of each branch make a circle. Tell students, "I know I have two flavors. Chocolate ice cream I can put in either a sugar cone or waffle cone, so I fill in these smaller circles with 'sugar' and 'waffle' because I can have chocolate in a sugar cone or chocolate in a waffle cone. Now, I do the same for vanilla. How many combinations are possible all together? What are they?" (*Four combinations; chocolate in a sugar cone, chocolate in a waffle cone, vanilla in a sugar cone, vanilla in a waffle cone*)

Say, "The tree diagram shows us how many combinations are possible and what they are. It's a useful way to organize information that leads to combinations." Pass out a copy of the tree diagram (p. 69) and the combos table (p. 70) to each student. Explain, "What Mr. Fairplay is asking for is the blank tree diagram filled in with the drink and snack choices listed in his letter. When that is done he is asking for that same information to be listed in the table. I can see he has also listed some abbreviations for the words, so feel free to use them."

Assign partners or have students work individually as you guide. When work is completed, review together.

ACTIVITY: **Making Your Own Tree Diagram**

Provide each student with a piece of drawing paper, pencil, and ruler. Tell them, "Now that you have made a tree diagram for Mr. Fairplay's snack stand, it is time for you to create your own. Choose some snacks and drinks that you would like to combine and make a tree diagram that shows all the possible combinations for your special snack stand. Feel free to add some illustrations and enticing names to your delicious food choices." These are fun for students to draw and make an interesting class display when completed.

Part 2: Probability

Materials

For each student:
- Probability Cartoons (p. 76)
- Practice Page #10 (p. 77)
- Review Page #10 (p. 78)
- pencil

For each group of 3–5 students:
- Letter #10 (p. 73)
- Dataville Activity Card #1: The Chances Are . . . (p. 74)
- The Chances Are . . . Record Sheet (p. 75)

For teacher demonstration:
- small paper bag
- six marbles of the same color and one of a different color
- small paper bags with the following 1 inch square colored construction paper pieces distributed as follows:
  Bag #1 = 5 red and 2 blue,
  Bag #2 = 7 red and 3 blue,
  Bag #3 = 4 red and 9 blue,
  Bag #4 = 7 red and 5 blue,
  Bag #5 = 1 red and 9 blue,
  Bag #6 = 9 red and 1 blue

ACTIVITY LESSON #10

What's in the Bag?

(UNDERSTANDING PROBABILITY)

> **Objective:** Students are introduced to probability, an area of mathematics that deals with chance. The terms *probably, likely, not likely, certain* and *impossible* are introduced.

Tell the class, "I have just received another letter and package of materials from Dataville." Allow students time to read the letter silently then read aloud together.

Say, "In his letter Mr. Fairplay uses the word 'probability.' What is probability?" Discuss possible definitions. Conclude along the lines of, "Probability is the mathematical study of chance or how likely things are to happen."

Say, "This morning I listened to the radio to hear people discuss the probability of something happening today. It helped me decide what to wear. What do you think it was?" *(Weather report or forecast)* Continue, "People who predict the weather have to think about the probability of something happening. For example, how likely it is to rain? They look at data from the past and the current conditions and make a prediction about what will happen, based on the probability."

Say, "Understanding probability helps us make predictions. For example, here is an empty bag. I am going to put these six green marbles in." (Use any color, but only one.)

Drop marbles in and shake bag. Say, "Without looking, I will reach in and take one marble out of the bag. What are the chances that the marble will be green?" The children will probably tell you that it definitely will be green. Ask, "Are you *certain* that it will be green?" *(Yes!)* "What does certain mean?" *(That it must happen)*

Ask, "Why?" *(Because all of the marbles are green. There are no other possibilities.)* Take a marble out and show that it is indeed green.

Add one red (color can vary) marble to the bag and say, "Now when I reach into the bag, is it still certain I will get a green marble?" *(No, because now there is a chance you could get a red one.)* Ask, "Is it more likely I will get a green or more likely I will get a red?" *(It is more likely to a get a green because there are more greens than red.)*

Say, "Let's try it." Ask eight or nine children to randomly pull out a marble one at a time. Each marble must be returned to the bag before the next child chooses. Make a table on the board or on chart paper, marking one column red and the other green. Use tally marks to indicate the result of each "pick." (Note: The more "picks" the more likely the theoretical probability will result.) Say, "Look at the results on the table. If you predicted green would be pulled out more often, you were right. You used probability to make a prediction."

Take all of the marbles out of the bag again. Ask, "How many possible results are there? (*7, 6 green and 1 red*) Out of the seven possible results, how many chances are there that you will pick a green?" (*6*) "So you have a six out of seven chance of picking a green. If this is so, what is the chance that you will pick a red?" (*1 out of 7*) Say, "We say that this result is *not likely or unlikely*." Make sure the children understand that even if a result is *not likely or unlikely*, it is not impossible.

Now put the seven marbles back in the bag and shake the bag. Ask, "What is the chance that I will pick a blue marble if I reach into the bag without looking?" (*You cannot pick a blue marble because there are no blue marbles in the bag.*) Say, "Picking a blue marble would be impossible. If there is no chance of something happening we can say it is impossible."

Pass out a copy of Dataville Activity Card #1 (p. 74) and The Chances Are . . . Record Sheet (p. 75) to each student. Put the students into groups of 3–5. Give each group a lunch bag with colored squares. Have them complete the activity as explained on the card. While the children are working with the activity, walk around to each group asking questions that will allow you to assess their understanding of the concept.

ACTIVITY: **Probability Cartoons**

To help students solidify their understanding of key probability words and phrases, give them an opportunity to do some probability cartoons. This activity incorporates math, language arts, and some creative drawing. It can be done in class or as a homework assignment. The Probability Cartoons page (p. 76) can be used to practice these particular words: *likely, unlikely, certain,* and *impossible.* For each word, students need to write the word in a sentence and draw an accompanying cartoon demonstrating that they understand its meaning. For example, a sentence for *likely* might be "It is likely he will pick a banana." The accompanying drawing could be of a hand

Teaching Tip
. . . .
Centers and Labs

Over these next few lessons, students will be introduced to a variety of probability games and activities. One format for practicing probability ideas is to organize these games and activities as stations, centers, or labs that students may work on independently or in a group rotation over a few days. In this way you will be able to circulate and observe students working on the concepts and students will enjoy a variety of experiences while practicing important skills and understandings.

Literature Link

*Pigs At Odds: Fun With
Math and Games*
by Amy Axelrod
(Simon and Schuster, 2000)

The Pig family enjoys a variety of games of chance at the county fair, making this book a good springboard for a discussion about probability found in common games.

Materials

For each student:

• one coin

• Dataville Activity Card #2:
  Heads or Tails (p. 74)

• Heads or Tails Record Sheet
  (p. 79)

• pencil

reaching into a bag that has 5 bananas and 1 orange. Any probability words that you want to practice can be reviewed in this same format. Remind students to use sentences that show understanding of the probability word. A sentence like, "Likely is a word that has six letters" does not show the writer understands the word.

ACTIVITY LESSON #11

It's a Toss-Up
(PROBABILITY WITH COINS)

> Objective: Students will examine the probability in a simple coin toss and how a previous toss does not determine or effect the next toss.

Begin by asking students, " Have you ever tossed a coin for anything?" Discuss examples such as determining who would go first in a game, in football who receives the kickoff, and other events from real life.

Ask, "How many possible results are there?" (*Two, heads or tails*) Then ask, "Which result is more likely?" (*Neither, because it is just as likely to land on one side as the other*) Write the two possible results on the board or chart paper. Toss the penny. Mark the result. Ask, "What are the chances that it will land on the same side on the second toss?" (*Listen to students' ideas and discuss. Some students may respond that it is more likely that the opposite side will come up, but the reality is that the chances are always 1 out of 2 or 50/50.*)

Say, "Today you will get to try the second probability game from Dataville. This will give you a chance to try out the probability ideas about a coin that we just discussed." Pass out a copy of Activity Card #2 (p. 74) to each student. Tell students, "Try to do as many tosses as possible during the class. The more data, the better. For fun, try to predict what the toss will be and compare your predictions to the actual results.

Have the students complete the Heads or Tails Record Sheet. Discuss the results at the end. You may want to combine individual results into a larger class result chart.

ACTIVITY: **Double Coin Toss**

If you would like to pursue this idea further, and combine it with a simple tree diagram, you may want to try this activity. Review the previous activity by asking, "How many possible results were there when we tossed the penny?" (*Two heads or tails*) Ask, "What was the chance that the penny would land on heads?" (*1 out of 2*) Ask also, "What was the chance that the penny would land on tails?" (*1 out of 2*)

Continue, "What would happen if we tossed two pennies at the same time? How many possible outcomes would we have?" (*You may ask a student to draw a simple tree diagram to show the possible results/outcomes. There are four possible results: heads – heads, heads – tails, tails – tails, and tails – heads.*)

Say, "Try the same activity we did yesterday, only this time use two coins and record your predictions and results." When completed, discuss the results and keep in mind that each penny can land heads or tails, so tails – heads and heads – tails each have the possibility of occurring. So when we look at the "chances" of each result, we say that there is a 1 out of 4 chance that they will both be heads, a 1 out of 4 chance that they will both be tails, and a 2 out of 4 chance that one will be heads and one will be tails. If the students understand this concept, they should be able to tell you that a one head and one tail result will be the *most likely* to occur.

ACTIVITY LESSON #12

Let's Take a Spin

(*PROBABILITY WITH SPINNERS*)

Objective: Students will examine probability concepts involved when using spinners.

Say to the class, "We have been learning about probability. One place probability appears a great deal is in games. Can you name any games you have played that have probability in them?" (*Students will mention various games. When a game with a spinner is mentioned, focus on that.*)

Draw a circle on the board. Draw a line to divide the circle in half. Shade in one half. Draw a spinner arrow on it. Say, "Pretend this is a real spinner and you and I are playing a game. If I spin the spinner

Video Connection

Math Talk: Take a Chance
Children's Television
Workshop, 1995

This video offers some excellent demonstrations of probability in the context of games. It uses humor, cartoons, and live action to make concepts of probability very clear. The sequence on the coin toss will reinforce the ideas in the lesson above. This is an idea that runs counterintuitive to the beliefs of many children, so it is worthwhile to see it presented in another way.

Materials

For each student:
- Practice Page #11/#12 (pp. 82 and 83)
- Review Page #11/#12 (p. 84)
- pencil

For each pair of students:
- Dataville Activity Card #3: Very SPINteresting! (p. 74)
- Very SPINteresting! Record Sheet (p. 80)
- Make Your Own Spinners (p. 81)
- a set of crayons; red, yellow, green, and blue
- 2 paper clips and 2 brass fasteners

Teaching Tip

Spinners

It is recommended that spinners be copied onto card stock paper for durability. There are two levels of spinners. Choose either the 4 possibilities or 8 possibilities, but the fair and unfair spinner should have the same number of possibilities. When using the unfair spinner in Activity Card #3, all 4 color results are marked on the record sheet and all four colors will not be used on the 4 possibility spinner. Use this opportunity to reinforce the concept of "impossible" as a result.

Materials

For each pair of students:
- Letter #13 (p. 85)
- Dice Roll Record Sheet (p. 86)
- pair of dice
- pencil

and it lands on the shaded part, I win. If it lands on the unshaded part, you win. Would that be fair? Why or why not?" (*Yes, it is fair, because each possible result on the spinner has the same chance of occurring. Both players have an equal, or 1 out of 2 or 50/50, chance of winning.*)

Now redraw the spinner on the board so 3/4 is shaded and 1/4 is unshaded. Say, "I've changed the spinner a little, but I'd still like to play the game the same way. If it lands on the shaded part, I win. If it lands on the unshaded part, you win. Is it still a fair game? Why or why not? (*No, it is not fair because there is a greater chance of landing on the shaded part.*)

Ask, "What are the chances of my winning?" (*Very likely, most likely, 3 out of 4*) Demonstrate to students how your chances could be written as a fraction. (*3/4, or 3 out of 4 while their chances would only be 1/4, or 1 our of 4*)

Tell students, "Today you are going to work with the third probability activity card from Mr. Fairplay." Pass out a copy of Activity Card #3 (p. 74) to each student. Read and review the directions together. Summarize the task saying, "So basically you will be creating two spinners, one fair spinner and one unfair spinner. You will predict what you think your results will be, then spin them and record the results to test your predictions." It is a good idea to pair students for this activity, so one partner can spin while the other records results. When the activity is complete, have students share their results with the class.

ACTIVITY LESSON #13

On A Roll
(*Probability With Dice*)

Objective: Students will examine the probability of rolling the possible sums on a pair of dice

Tell students, "Last time we looked at probability with spinners. We also mentioned how spinners are used to include an element of chance in games. What other tool is used in games to make chance a part of the game? (*dice*) Ask, "Do you know any games that use dice?" Discuss student responses.

Say, "We have a letter here from Mr. Fairplay that mentions some problems they were having with a game that used dice. Let's read it and see what we think." Give each student a copy of letter (p. 85). Allow time to read silently, then read aloud and discuss.

Summarize, "So Mr. Fairplay wants you to do some research and make some recommendations. You will have to roll the dice as many times as possible during this class period and record the sum of each roll on the record sheet. Partner up so one person can roll the dice while the other can record the roll. You can switch jobs every ten rolls or so. Remember, the more rolls you make, the better your data will be. Don't forget to record the sum that came up the most and answer the question that asks why you think that happened, as well as providing Mr. Fairplay with your recommendations for the game."

When students have completed the task, meet to share results and discuss. Students will find that the sum of seven is the most likely sum to come up because there are six different ways to create the sum of seven with the dice. It is the only sum that can be made that many ways, so it has the greatest possibility of occurring.

Activity: Combinations Chart

As students write their answers to Mr. Fairplay, explaining their thinking, they may want to chart out the combinations that are possible as follows:

Sum	Combinations
2	(1 + 1)
3	(2 + 1), (1 + 2)
4	(2 + 2), (1 + 3), (3 + 1)
5	(3 + 2), (2 + 3), (4 + 1), (1 + 4)
6	(3 + 3), (4 + 2), (2 + 4), (5 + 1), (1 + 5)
7	(4 + 3), (3 + 4), (6 + 1), (1 + 6), (5 + 2), (2 + 5)
8	(4 + 4), (6 + 2), (2 + 6), (3 + 5), (5 + 3)
9	(4 + 5), (5 + 4), (6 + 3), (3 + 6)
10	(5 + 5), (6 + 4), (4 + 6)
11	(5 + 6), (6 + 5)
12	(6 + 6)

This helps students visualize the probabilities for each sum based on the possible combinations that create that sum.

Teaching Tip

The More the Better

Rolling dice is a good activity to help students see the importance of doing numerous trials before making statements about data. If we were to roll two dice once and get a sum of 12, could we conclude that 12 is the most likely sum to occur? Only when dice are rolled many, many times can we get an accurate picture of the probability of these events. This is true for most investigations of probability and the resulting predictions. The more data the better.

Literature Link

Jumanji by Chris Van Allsburg (Houghton Mifflin, 1981)

Beautifully illustrated classic picture book about a game that has incredible outcomes for the brother and sister who find it in the park. With each roll of the dice, another amazing event occurs as the children battle to survive.

Materials

For each student:

• Letter #14 (p. 87)

• Pick and Place Record Sheet (p. 88)

• Pick and Place Board (p. 89)

• pencil

• Practice Page #13/#14 (p. 91)

• Review Page #13/#14 (p. 92)

For each pair of students:

• Set of digit cards (p. 90)

Teaching Tip

Encouragement and Reward

At the culmination of the data analysis and probability tasks presented in this book, you may want to consider a final reward for all the students, in honor of their dedication to relearning and mastering these challenging skills. A simple celebration that includes snacks or treats that come in various colors—such as grapes, fish-shaped snack crackers, gum drops, or jelly beans—might inspire some data-related or probability experiments!

ACTIVITY LESSON #14

Probability Pick and Place
(PROBABILITY WITH NUMBER CARDS)

> Objective: Students will investigate the probability of getting certain numbers from a deck of digit cards as they play a game with a partner.

Begin by saying, "We have another letter from Mr. Fairplay." Pass out a copy of Letter #14 (p. 87). Have students read the letter silently, then read aloud together. Summarize by saying, "So Mr. Fairplay would like you to test out this game. I'll play it once with a partner to demonstrate. Then you can try it out with a partner of your own."

Sit with a partner so all students can see you work. Each of you should have a recording sheet, pencil, and Pick and Place Board. Shuffle the deck of digit cards and put the deck face-down between you and your partner. Tell students, "My partner and I are going to take turns picking a card from the deck. Once we make the pick, we must place the card on the Pick and Place Board. Once the card is placed you can't move it. The object of the game is to create the largest possible odd, four-digit number."

Play one or two rounds with your partner. Remember at the end of each round to record the final numbers. Ask students, "How can I be sure to get an odd number?" (Place an odd digit card in the "ones" place of the Pick and Place Board) Then ask, "What are my chances of getting an odd number when the game begins?" *(10 out of 20 or 50/50)*

Have students play the game and then answer Mr. Fairplay's question about the game and probability on their own. Discuss these answers as a class.

Name: _____ Date: _____

What is your favorite _____?

Survey by: _____

Directions: _____

_____

_____

Choices	Responses

Name: _____ Date: _____

What I Have Learned From the Data

Topic or name of survey

_____

I have analyzed the data and this is what I know:

_____

_____

_____

_____

_____

_____

_____

_____

_____

_____

_____

_____

Name: _____ Date: _____

Reteaching Math: Data Analysis & Probability © 2008 by Bob Krech, Scholastic Teaching Resources

WORD PROBLEM

The third graders at Skillmaster Elementary School convinced the principal to replace the old soda machine with a new healthy beverage machine. The students have come up with seven healthy beverages that they would like, however, this new machine can only hold five different beverages. How can the students decide which beverages would be most popular with the students in the entire school?

BASICS BOX

data-information survey: a process where a group of people are asked the same question

analyze: to look carefully at data or a situation and make conclusions

The third graders can create a survey to help them collect data.

Healthy Beverage Survey

Directions: Please choose 5 of the following beverages that you would like to see offered in the new beverage machine. Use tally marks to mark your choices.

Milk	
Water	
Veggie Juice	
Pineapple Juice	
Apple Juice	
Orange Juice	
Tomato Juice	

After students have marked their choices, the third graders can analyze the data. The 5 beverages with the most votes can be ordered for the new machine.

PRACTICE

The manager of Fred's Fish Shop decided to see how many of each type of fish were sold in the shop during one week. He created the following survey to collect the data. Analyze the data on the survey and answer the questions.

Fish Sold During the Week of May 4th	
Goldfish	⊥⊥⊥⊥ ⊥⊥⊥⊥ ⊥⊥⊥⊥ ⊥⊥⊥⊥ ⊥⊥⊥⊥ ⊥⊥⊥⊥
Angel Fish	⊥⊥⊥⊥ ⊥⊥⊥⊥ ⊥⊥⊥⊥ II
Zebra Fish	⊥⊥⊥⊥ ⊥⊥⊥⊥ ⊥⊥⊥⊥ II
Discus Fish	⊥⊥⊥⊥ ⊥⊥⊥⊥ I
Cardinal Tetras	⊥⊥⊥⊥ ⊥⊥⊥⊥
Swordtail Fish	⊥⊥⊥⊥ ⊥⊥⊥⊥ ⊥⊥⊥⊥ ⊥⊥⊥⊥ II

1. Which type of fish sold the most? _____

2. How many fish were sold all together? _____

3. If Fred decided to only sell four types of fish, which would you recommend? Why? _____

_____

JOURNAL

Create a short survey about food and try it with the people in your home or with your friends. Record the data and analyze it.

29

Name: _____   Date: _____

Surveys and Data

Analyze the data on each survey to answer the questions.

1. How many visitors came to the Fall Festival? _____

2. Were most visitors Return Visitors or First Time Visitors?

   _____

Fall Festival Visitors	
First Time Visitors	ⵏⵏ ⵏⵏ ⵏⵏ ⵏⵏ ⵏⵏ ⵏⵏ ⵏⵏ l
Return Visitors	ⵏⵏ ⵏⵏ ⵏⵏ ⵏⵏ ⵏⵏ ⵏⵏ ⵏⵏ ⵏⵏ ⵏⵏ ⵏⵏ ⵏⵏ lll

3. Which sport is the favorite? _____

4. How many did not choose basketball? _____

Favorite Indoor Sports	
Wrestling	✔ ✔ ✔
Soccer	✔ ✔ ✔ ✔
Basketball	✔ ✔
Gymnastics	✔ ✔ ✔
Floor Hockey	✔ ✔ ✔ ✔ ✔

5. Did more readers read humor or adventure?

   _____

6. Which readers read both nonfiction and mysteries?

   _____

Books Read During the Summer	
Nonfiction	Miguel Stanley Rita Beth Matt Jasmine
Animal Stories	Jasmine Liz Rob Beth Debra Max Noah
Humor	Jackie Callie Mike Rick Liam
Adventure	Matt Stanley Rita Walt
Mysteries	Rita Jasmine Matt

7. Which type of book was read by the least number of readers? _____

8. Which readers read the most books? _____

Reteaching Math: Data Analysis & Probability © 2008 by Bob Krech, Scholastic Teaching Resources

County of Dataville 13th Annual Games Fair

Dear Students,

Greetings from the County of Dataville. Each year we ask a group of students to join us in collecting, recording, organizing, and analyzing data for our Annual Games Fair. By doing this we get to have organized records for each of our Annual Games Fairs while students who help get to strengthen their skills in data analysis and probability. I am honored that you will be helping us this year.

This year we have eight towns participating in the fair. Each town has completed an application indicating which games they will participate in. Enclosed is a table showing the names of the towns and the games they want to play. Each town is allowed to play in up to four games.

I would like to show how many teams are participating in each sport. Please organize the data once on a pictograph and then again on a bar graph. I have enclosed everything that you will need to make the pictograph and bar graph as well as a question sheet for you to fill in after you analyze the data.

I look forward to working with you.

Sincerely,

Bruce B. Fairplay

Dataville Games Chairman
Dataville, USA

Name: _____ Date: _____

County of Dataville 13th Annual Games Fair Table of Sports Competition Participation

Town	Soccer	Bowling	Volleyball	Baseball	Basketball
Brook Point	1	1		1	1
Marshtown	1	1	1		1
Waterton	1		1		1
Stream Valley	1	1	1	1	
Lakeland	1		1	1	1
Fountain Woods	1	1		1	1
River Valley	1		1	1	1
Canal Run	1		1		

Reteaching Math: Data Analysis & Probability © 2008 by Bob Krech, Scholastic Teaching Resources

Name: _____ Date: _____

County of Dataville 13th Annual Games Fair Table of Sports Competition Participation: Pictograph

Soccer	Bowling	Volleyball	Baseball	Basketball

Name: _____   Date: _____

Pictograph Pieces

Name: _____ Date: _____

County of Dataville 13ᵗʰ Annual Games Fair Table of Sports Competition Participation: Bar Graph

	Soccer	Bowling	Volleyball	Baseball	Basketball
13					
12					
11					
10					
9					
8					
5					
6					
5					
4					
3					
2					
1					

Use the pictograph and bar graph that you completed to answer the following questions.

1. Which sport will have the most participation? _____

2. Are more towns participating in baseball or basketball?

   _____

3. How many more teams are participating in volleyball than in bowling? _____

4. Which sport will have the least participation? _____

5. How many towns are participating in both soccer and bowling?

   _____

6. Which two sports have the same amount of participation?

   _____

Name: _____ Date: _____

Reteaching Math: Data Analysis & Probability © 2008 by Bob Krech, Scholastic Teaching Resources

WORD PROBLEM

The pictograph show the snacks that were brought in on Tuesday. If every child was present and brought a snack, how many children are in the class?

Tuesday Snacks

Banana   Cookie   Apple

BASICS BOX

Organized data is easier to analyze and understand.

A **pictograph** is a graph that uses pictures or symbols to represent data.

A **bar graph** uses labeled horizontal or vertical bars that show different values. The numbers along a side of a bar graph are called the **scale**.

The pictograph shows that 3 children brought bananas, 2 brought cookies and 4 brought apples for snack. Adding these together, we know that there are nine children in the class.

A bar graph can show the same information in another way.

PRACTICE

Use the pictograph to complete the bar graph. Use the graphs to answer the questions below.

Favorite Pies

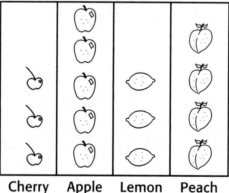

Cherry   Apple   Lemon   Peach

Favorite Pies

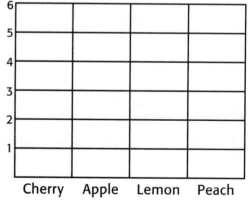

Cherry   Apple   Lemon   Peach

1. How many people chose peach as their favorite pie? _____

2. How many people did not choose lemon as their favorite? _____

3. What is the most popular type of pie? _____

4. How many people answered the survey? _____

36

Name: _____   Date: _____

Use the registration information for Mac's Cool Camp for Kids from the pictograph and bar graph to answer the questions.

Activity Registration

Canoe Race	● ● ● ●
Bike Hike	● ● ● ● ●
Wood Craft	● ● ●
Swim Relay	● ● ● ● ● ● ● ●

Each ● = 5 campers

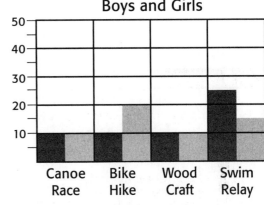

Activity Registration: Boys and Girls

Canoe Race   Bike Hike   Wood Craft   Swim Relay

Boys   Girls

1. Which activity has the most girls participating? _____

2. How many boys are registered for this week of camp? _____

3. Ten campers at a time can participate in a bike hike. If all
    of the children who registered for the bike hike have a turn,
    how many bike hikes will there need to be? _____

4. Which graph could be used to answer all of the questions? Explain. _____
    _____

Explain when and why it is helpful to have a picture symbol represent more than one thing.

Name: _____ Date: _____

Pictographs and Bar Graphs

Put the data from the pictograph onto the bar graph.

Look at the bar graph. Answer the questions.

1. How many swimmers are on the 10-year-olds' team? _____

2. How many more 13-year-olds than 15-year-olds? _____

3. What is the youngest age group? _____

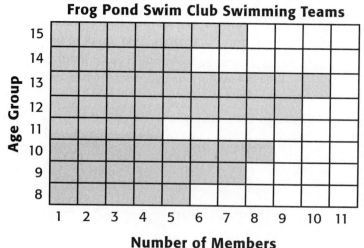

Look at the bar graph. Answer the questions.

4. On which day were the most cups of lemonade sold? _____

5. What were the three top-selling days? _____

6. Were more cups in total sold on weekend days or weekdays? _____

Lemonade Sales

Sunday	🥤🥤🥤🥤🥤
Monday	🥤🥤
Tuesday	🥤🥤🥤
Wednesday	🥤🥤🥤🥤
Thursday	🥤🥤🥤
Friday	🥤🥤
Saturday	🥤🥤🥤🥤🥤🥤

Each 🥤 **= 10 cups**

38

Reteaching Math: Data Analysis & Probability © 2008 by Bob Krech, Scholastic Teaching Resources

County of Dataville 13th Annual Games Fair

Dear Students,

Once again, I send greetings from the county of Dataville. The games are well underway and the participation and sportsmanship have been outstanding!

We have just finished the bowling portion of our games and have enclosed the scores for each participating team.

I would like you to analyze the line plots that display the scores for the individual teams. Each mark indicates the average score for each player. Please complete the enclosed Results of the Bowling Competition table which will become part of the detailed records we keep.

I would also like you to combine all of the data onto one single line plot. I have enclosed longer strips of paper to make this task easier. Afterwards, please analyze the combined line plot and answer the enclosed questions.

I truly appreciate your help in compiling our records and hope that you develop a strong understanding of line plots.

Sincerely,

Bruce B. Fairplay

Dataville Games Chairman
Dataville, USA

Reteaching Math: Data Analysis & Probability © 2008 by Bob Krech, Scholastic Teaching Resources

Name: _____   Date: _____

County of Dataville 13th Annual Games Fair
Bowling Competition Results

* Each ● indicates the average score of one bowler.

Brook Point

140	141	142	143	144	145	146	147	148	149
●	●	●●			●		●		●

Marshtown

145	146	147	148	149	150	151	152	153	154
●		●			●		●●●		●

Stream Valley

147	148	149	150	151	152	153	154	155	156
		●●			●		●	●	●●

Fountain Woods

153	154	155	156	157	158	159	160	161	162
			●●●	●		●	●		●

Reteaching Math: Data Analysis & Probability © 2008 by Bob Krech, Scholastic Teaching Resources

Name: _____   Date: _____

County of Dataville 13th Annual Games Fair
Bowling Competition Results Analysis

Results are for individual teams.

	Brook Point	Marshtown	Stream Valley	Fountain Woods
How many bowlers were on the team?				
How many bowlers scored 150 or higher?				
What was the lowest score?				
What was the highest score?				
Find the range for each team.				

Name: _____   Date: _____

County of Dataville 13th Annual Games Fair
Combined Bowling Results

1. How many bowlers participated in the bowling event? _____

2. How many bowlers had a score of 150 or more? _____

3. What was the highest score? _____

4. What was the lowest score? _____

5. What was the range? _____

6. Using sentences, list 3 other things you know after analyzing the data.

   _____

   _____

   _____

   _____

   _____

   _____

   _____

   _____

Reteaching Math: Data Analysis & Probability © 2008 by Bob Krech, Scholastic Teaching Resources

Name: _____ Date: _____

WORD PROBLEM

Marcus has drawn a line plot to organize and display data from his team's recent free throw shooting contest. Each child had 10 tosses. The line plot shows the total baskets (out of 10 tries) that each child made. How many children made 5 or more baskets? What was the range of the data?

```
      X                       X
      X                       X
      X           X       X   X           X   X
  X   X           X       X   X           X   X
──────────────────────────────────────────────
  0   1   2   3   4   5   6   7   8   9   10
```

BASICS BOX

Line plots are a way to organize data. They are best used when the highest and lowest numbers are fairly close. The numbers are evenly spaced below a horizontal line. A mark is made above each number to show a result.

In the line plot, you can see that 2 children got 5 baskets, 4 children got 7 baskets, 2 children got 9 baskets, and 2 children got 10 baskets. So by adding them together you find the answer:

$2 + 4 + 2 + 2 = 10$ children

10 children made 5 or more baskets.

Range is the difference between the lowest and highest result.

Range can be calculated by subtracting the lowest number from the highest number. The difference is the range.

Since the highest result on the line plot is 10 and the lowest result is 0, you can use subtraction to find the answer:

$10 - 0 = 10$

The range is 10.

PRACTICE

Toss a die 12 times. Record the number that lands face up. Record the data in this table and use it to create your line plot below.

1	2	3	4	5	6

JOURNAL

How is a line plot similar to a bar graph and how it is different?

Name: _____   Date: _____

Line Plots and Range

Children collected cans of dog food for the local animal shelter. This line plot shows how many cans each child collected.

```
                                                          x
                                                          x
                                                          x
                                       x          x       x  x              x
                                       x     x    x       x  x        x  x
          x                      x     x     x  x  x  x  x  x  x  x  x  x
 ───────────────────────────────────────────────────────────────────────────
 23  24  25  26  27  28  29  30  31  32  33  34  35  36  37  38  39  40  41  42  43  44  45  46  47  48  49  50
```

1. How many children collected cans? _____

2. What was the highest number of cans collected? _____

3. What was the most common number of cans collected? _____

4. How many children collected between 40 and 50 cans? _____

5. What was the range of the data? _____

Twenty-four children took a Math test. Mark the scores on the line plot. Here are their scores:

96, 93, 88, 78, 88, 98, 88, 93, 84, 88, 96, 98, 95, 96, 93, 93, 88, 84, 92, 92, 95, 88, 97, 94

```
 ───────────────────────────────────────────────────────────────────────────
 77  78  79  80  81  82  83  84  85  86  87  88  89  90  91  92  93  94  95  96  97  98
```

6. What is the lowest score? _____

7. What is the most common score? _____

8. How many scores are lower than 89? _____

9. What is the range of the data? _____

Name: _____   Date: _____

History of High and Low Bowling Scores

The highest team scores were achieved during the 10th Annual Games Fair by the Fountain Woods Team. The following line plots shows the scores:

(2)				(3)			(1)		(1)	(1)	(2)
265	266	267	268	269	270	271	272	273	274	275	276

1. Range = _____

2. Mean = _____

3. Median = _____

4. Mode = _____

The lowest team scores were achieved during the 3rd Annual Games Fair by the Marshtown team. The following line plots shows the scores:

(1)					(2)		(1)	(1)
113	114	115	116	117	118	119	120	121

5. Range = _____

6. Mean = _____

7. Median = _____

8. Mode = _____

Reteaching Math: Data Analysis & Probability © 2008 by Bob Krech, Scholastic Teaching Resources

Name: _____ Date: _____

Crusty's Pie Shop sponsors a pie eating contest every year. This year nine contestants sat down to eat as many fruit pies as they could in six minutes. This table shows the results of the contest. Find the mean, median, mode, and range for the results.

Contestant	Pies Eaten
Big Bob	12
Hungry Harv	16
Mighty Mike	16
Tiny Tom	10
Big Bite Bart	18
Fed Up Frank	16
Lip-licking Lou	20
Some More Sue	19
Never Enough Nelly	17

BASICS BOX

The **mean** is the average of a set of numbers. To calculate the mean, find the total sum of the numbers and divide it by the number of addends.

The **median** is the number that falls in the middle when the numbers are in order from least to greatest.

The **mode** is the number that occurs most often.

Range is the difference between the highest and lowest numbers.

In the pie eating contest the **mean** is 16 because 12 + 16 + 16 + 10 + 18 + 16 + 20 + 19 + 17 = 144. This sum when divided by 9 (the number of addends) equals 16.

The **median** is 16. We can see that when we arrange the numbers 10, 12, 16, 16, 16, 17, 18, 19, 20.

The **mode** is 16. We can see that 16 occurs three times in the data.

The **range** is 10 because 20 − 10 = 10.

PRACTICE Find the mean, median, mode, and range for each set of numbers.

1. 21, 28, 49, 63, 21, 35, 21
    mean = _____   mode = _____

    median = _____   range = _____

2. 36, 12, 30, 41, 36, 49
    mean = _____   mode = _____

    median = _____   range = _____

JOURNAL

Write a word problem containing a series of at least seven numbers.
Find the mean, median, mode, and range for the numbers in your problem.

Reteaching Math: Data Analysis & Probability © 2008 by Bob Krech, Scholastic Teaching Resources

Name: _____   Date: _____

Mean, Median, Mode

Find the mean for each set of numbers.

1. 5, 2, 6, 5, 3, 4, 3

mean = _____

2. 3, 6, 7, 5, 4

mean = _____

3. 3, 6, 7, 8, 5, 4, 6, 3, 5, 3

mean = _____

Find the mode (the number that occurs most often) for each set of numbers.

4. 33, 35, 37, 33, 37, 33, 39, 37, 33, 38, 35, 37, 38, 37

mode = _____

5. 117, 117, 119, 123, 124, 123, 124, 123, 135, 119, 123, 128, 119

mode = _____

6. 7, 12, 13, 48, 12, 12, 12, 48, 7, 7, 13, 13, 48, 13, 7, 13

mode = _____

Find the median (middle number in the series when arranged in numeric order) for each set of numbers.

7. 2, 8, 10, 6, 3, 8, 3, 12, 11

median = _____

8. 19, 32, 18, 33, 26, 24, 21, 18, 30, 27, 19

median = _____

9. 76, 67, 75, 57, 62, 76, 73, 62, 60

median = _____

Find the mean, mode, median, and range for this set of numbers.

10. 24, 31, 25, 40 45, 35, 24, 33, 23, 35, 45, 24

mean = _____   mode = _____

median = _____   range = _____

Reteaching Math: Data Analysis & Probability © 2008 by Bob Krech, Scholastic Teaching Resources

County of Dataville 13th Annual Games Fair

Dear Students,

Greetings! As the games continue, the county of Dataville could not feel prouder of this year's participants. Not only are our games running smoothly, but our statistical records have never been better. For this, I thank you!

As the chairman of the Annual Games Fair, I have always found it helpful to use Venn diagrams as a way to display data. I would like to include, in this year's records, several Venn diagrams that will make it easy to see which teams competed in the same events.

Of course, this is where you come in. Please use the enclosed Table of Sports Competition Participation to create the following Venn diagrams:

1. Bowling/Volleyball
2. Basketball/Volleyball
3. Baseball/Basketball

4. Volleyball/Baseball
5. Bowling/Baseball
6. Bowling/Basketball

I have enclosed blank Venn diagrams for you to use. Please remember to label each circle with the sport. Please write the name of each town in the correct area of the diagram.

If you feel ready for a challenge, please also create Venn diagrams that will take a look at three sports at the same time. I have enclosed some three-circle Venn diagrams for this purpose. Again, remember to label each circle with the correct sport.

1. Basketball/Baseball/Bowling

2. Volleyball/Soccer/Baseball

3. Basketball/Bowling/Soccer

I am sure that your completed Venn diagrams will be great. Our fair would not be the same without your help.

Sincerely,

Bruce B. Fairplay

Dataville Games Chairman
Dataville, USA

Reteaching Math: Data Analysis & Probability © 2008 by Bob Krech, Scholastic Teaching Resources

Name: _____ Date: _____

Two-Circle Venn Diagram

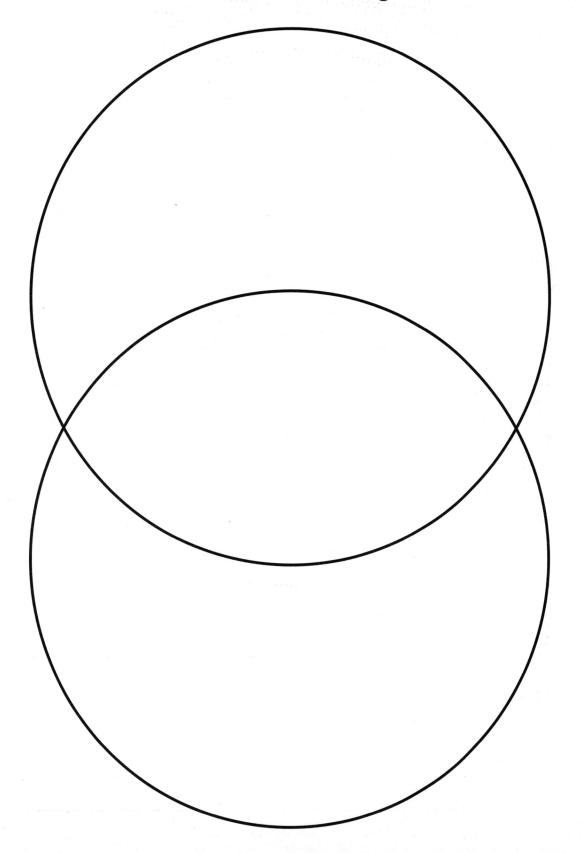

Name: _____   Date: _____

Three-Circle Venn Diagram

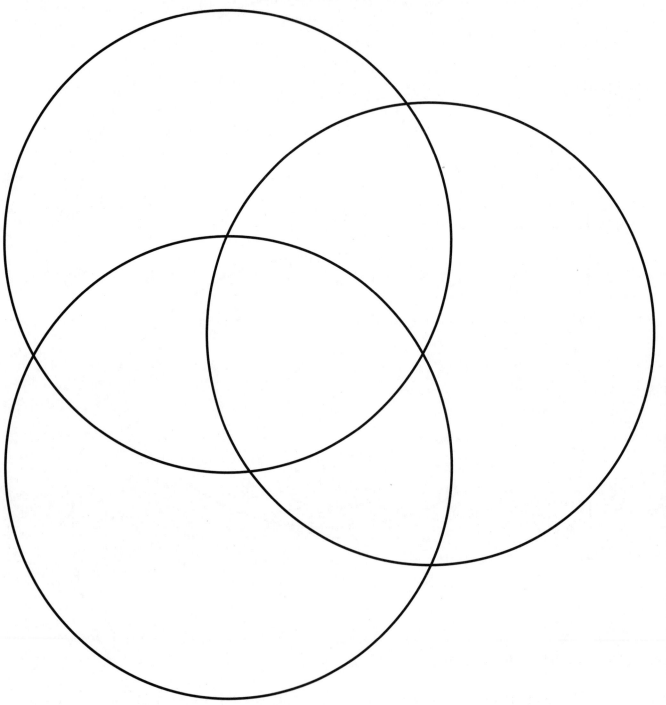

Reteaching Math: Data Analysis & Probability © 2008 by Bob Krech, Scholastic Teaching Resources

Name: _____   Date: _____

Reteaching Math: Data Analysis & Probability © 2008 by Bob Krech, Scholastic Teaching Resources

WORD PROBLEM

Each child in Rupert's Reptile club wrote his or her name in the correct place on this Venn diagram to indicate the pet or pets they own. How many club members own both a lizard and a snake?

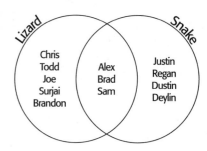

BASICS BOX

A **Venn diagram** is a graphic organizer made up of two or more overlapping circles to show relationships between sets. The similarities are placed in the overlapping areas while the differences are indicated in non-overlapping areas.

To figure out who owns both a lizard and a snake look in the overlapping area. Three names are in both circles and thus in the overlap area. They are Alex, Brad, and Sam.

PRACTICE

Use the data from this Venn diagram to answer the questions below.

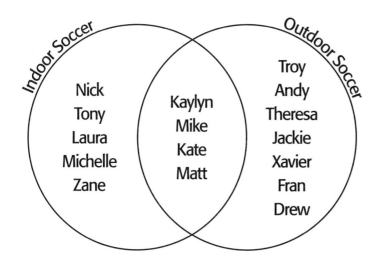

1. How many children play indoor soccer? _____

2. How many children play outdoor or indoor soccer (but not both)? _____

3. How many children play both indoor and outdoor soccer? _____

JOURNAL

Use the data below to complete a Venn diagram.

There are 11 members on the Freefall Dive team. Lucy, Miguel, Susan, Frank, Wanda, Chester, and Rex compete in the high dive competition. Susan, Rex, Andrew, Ryan, Frank, Betty, and Lewis compete in the stunt dive competition.

Name: _____ Date: _____

Venn Diagrams

Skating

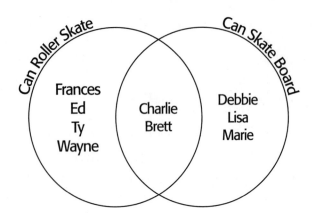

Traveling

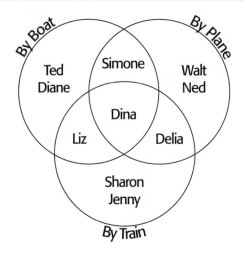

1. How many children can roller skate or ride a skate board?

   _____

2. Who can roller skate but cannot ride a skate board?

   _____

   _____

3. How many children can roller skate and ride a skate board?

   _____

4. Who can ride a skate board but cannot roller skate? _____

   _____

5. How many children have traveled by boat, plane, or train?

   _____

6. How many children have traveled by boat or train?

   _____

7. How many children have traveled by train only?

   _____

8. Which child has traveled by boat, train, and plane?

   _____

Reteaching Math: Data Analysis & Probability © 2008 by Bob Krech, Scholastic Teaching Resources

County of Dataville 13th Annual Games Fair

Dear Students,

As always, I send greetings from Dataville. One of the favorite events at the Annual Games Fair is the Pie Tasting Contest. This year we had the highest number of entries ever. Each year we like to record what types of pies were entered in the contest and what better way to record this data than with a pie chart!

Enclosed please find the Pie Entry pie charts for this year. We would like you to look at this chart and analyze the data. To make this more manageable, we have enclosed a sheet of questions for you to answer.

Thank you for all of your analyzing expertise. I hope this pie chart does not make you hungry!

Sincerely,

Bruce B. Fairplay

Dataville Games Chairman
Dataville, USA

P.S. Miss Emma Baker won the Pie Contest this year with her deep dish, cinnamon topped peach pie. It was simply splendid. Too bad it doesn't travel well by mail or we would have sent you a slice.

Reteaching Math: Data Analysis & Probability © 2008 by Bob Krech, Scholastic Teaching Resources

Name: _____   Date: _____

Dataville 13ᵗʰ Annual Pie Contest

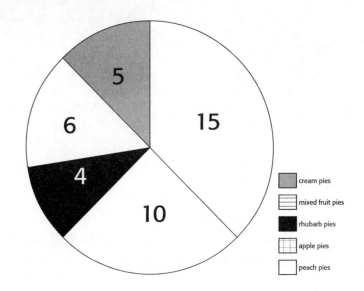

1. How many pies were entered in this year's contest? _____

2. Which flavor pie had the most entries? _____

3. How many of the pies were cream pies? _____

4. Which two pies together had the same amount of entries as the apple pie? _____

5. The total of rhubarb pie plus which two other pies made up exactly half of the pie entries?

_____

6. How many more peach pies than mixed fruit pies were entered in the contest? _____

7. How many pies were not apple?

_____

Fill in the blanks.

8. _____ out _____ of pies were apple pies.

9. _____ out _____ pies were peach pies.

10. _____ out _____ pies were rhubarb pies.

11. _____ out _____ pies were mixed fruit pies.

12. _____ out _____ pies were cream pies.

Reteaching Math: Data Analysis & Probability © 2008 by Bob Krech, Scholastic Teaching Resources

Name: _____   Date: _____

WORD PROBLEM

Lester earns $3.00 in allowance each week. He feels that he needs to earn more money and has drawn this pie chart to show his parents where the money will go. How much more money does Lester need to earn each week to have enough for his money plan?

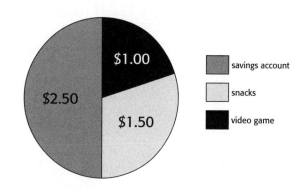

savings account

snacks

video game

BASICS BOX

A **pie chart** is used to show the relationship of all pieces of a whole. In Lester's case, the whole is the total amount of money he wants to earn each week. Each piece shows a specific way Lester wants to use some of the money. The size of the piece depends on how much of the total money he wants to use for that piece. The bigger the piece, the more money needed. If we add all of the pieces together, we will know how much money

Lester wants to earn each week.
$1.00 toward saving for a video game + $1.50 toward snack money + $2.50 toward his savings = $5.00

If Lester wants to earn $5.00 each week and he already earns $3.00 each week, he needs to earn $2.00 more each week for his money plan.

PRACTICE

This pie chart shows the different jobs students have in the school play. Use the pie chart to answer the questions.

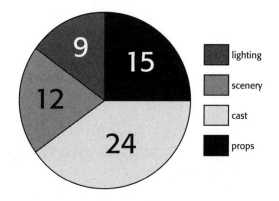

lighting

scenery

cast

props

1. How many students are in the cast? _____

2. How many students are working as the lighting crew? _____

3. Are more students on the lighting crew or on props? _____

4. How many children are designing scenery? _____

5. Are more students involved in the backstage activities or as characters in the cast? _____

Name: _____   Date: _____

PRACTICE

The children in Room #31 put together this pie chart to show their parents how much time they spend on activities during the school day. Use the pie chart to answer the questions.

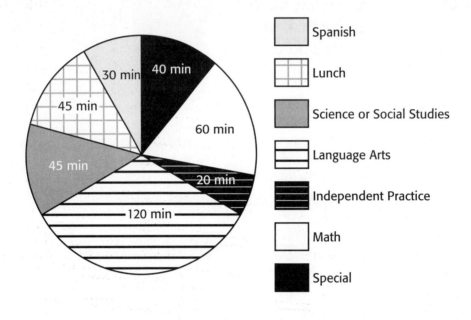

Spanish

Lunch

Science or Social Studies

Language Arts

Independent Practice

Math

Special

1. The most time is spent on which activity? _____

2. How much time is spent doing math? _____

3. Is more time spent on Spanish or Independent Practice? _____

4. Lunch has the same amount of time as? _____

5. How many minutes did the students include in their pie chart? _____

JOURNAL

How are all of the pieces of a pie chart related to each other?

Name: _____   Date: _____

Pie Charts

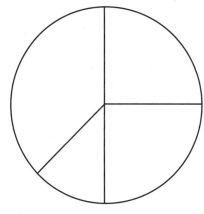

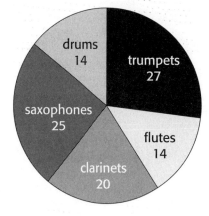

Vanessa's Allowance

Vanessa receives $20.00 allowance each month. Half of her money is split evenly between movies and bowling. She spends $3.00 on snacks and the rest goes into savings. Fill in the pie chart to show how Vanessa uses her allowance. Include amounts.

Junior Concert Band

1. How many musicians are in the Junior Concert Band? _____

2. How many more trumpet players than drummers? _____

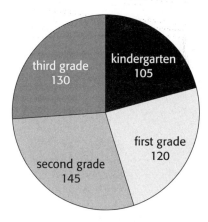

Monthly Pet Care

3. What is the biggest pet care expense? _____

4. What is the total pet care cost each month? _____

Enrollment at Dataville Elementary School

5. Which grade has the greatest amount of students? _____

6. Which grade has the least amount of students? _____

Name: _____   Date: _____

Fortieths Circle

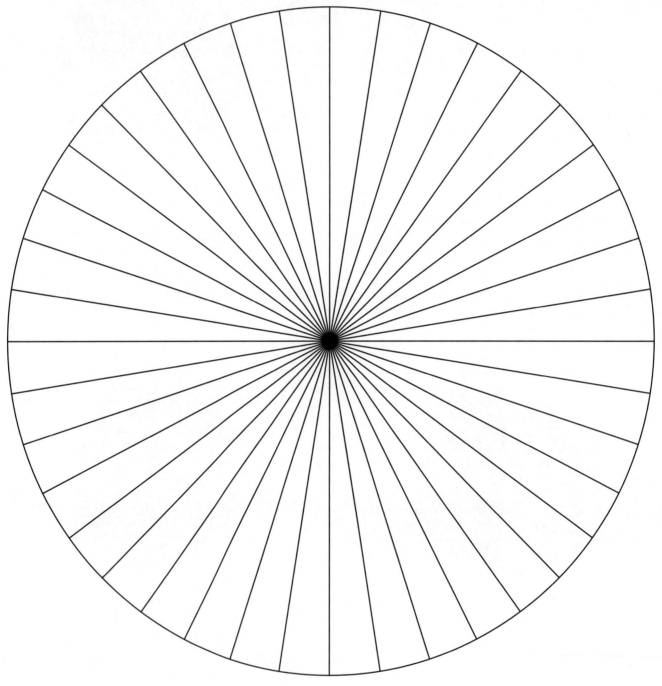

Reteaching Math: Data Analysis & Probability © 2008 by Bob Krech, Scholastic Teaching Resources

Name: _____   Date: _____

WORD PROBLEM

Magical Marvin spent the money in his savings account to start a magic show. This pie chart shows how he spent the money. What fraction of his money did he spend on costumes? Write the answer in lowest terms.

BASICS BOX

To determine what fractions of Marvin's money was spent on costumes, we first have to know how much money he spent all together. To find this, add all of the amounts. $25.00 + $25.00 + $50.00 = $100.00. $100.00 is the whole. When we look at the chart, we see that he spent $25.00 out of $100.00 on costumes.

So Marvin spent $\frac{25}{100}$ of his money on costumes. To reduce this to lowest terms, find the greatest number that divides evenly into both 25 and 100.

$$\frac{25}{25} = 1 \qquad \frac{100}{25} = 4$$

So Marvin spent $\frac{1}{4}$ of his money on costumes.

PRACTICE   Use a fraction to answer the question under each pie chart. Reduce each fraction to the lowest terms.

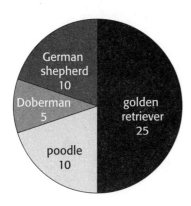

Favorite Dogs

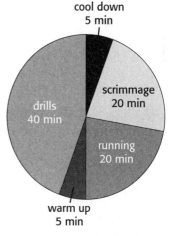

Soccer Practice Schedule

1. What fraction of people like Dobermans best? _____

2. What fraction of soccer practice is spent on drills? _____

JOURNAL

Explain in words and/or pictures what makes a pie chart a good way to compare parts of a whole.

Name: _____   Date: _____

Pie Chart Fractions

Write a fraction for the shaded part of each pie chart.

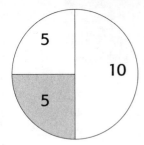

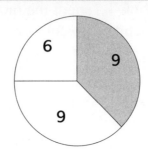

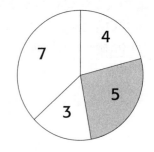

1. _____

2. _____

3. _____

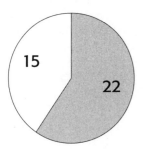

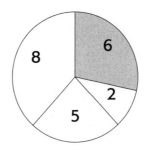

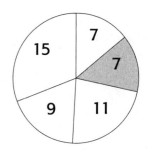

4. _____

5. _____

6. _____

Shade in the pie chart to match the fraction.

7.
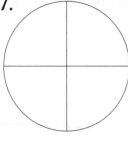

$$\frac{3}{4}$$

8.
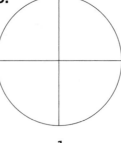

$$\frac{1}{4}$$

9.
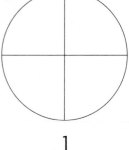

$$\frac{1}{2}$$

Reteaching Math: Data Analysis & Probability © 2008 by Bob Krech, Scholastic Teaching Resources

County of Dataville 13th Annual Games Fair

Dear Students,

Greetings once again from Dataville! Observing trends is a very important part of the decision-making here at the Annual Games Fair. We try to give the people what they want. Therefore, each year we put data on line graphs to give a clear picture of what areas of our games fair are most popular. One of the important line graphs that we look at each year is our attendance graph. We are pleased that the attendance has gone up each year. I have enclosed a copy of the line graph for our most recent five years. I would like you to look at this line graph and answer the questions under it.

Once you feel that you have a good understanding of how to read and analyze a line graph, I would like you to make a few additional line graphs for us. I have enclosed data tables for the sports participation, pie baking, and bowling contests. Please create a line graph for each one and write two statements listing things that you know after analyzing each graph.

Thank you and may all of the bar graphs in your education have positive trends.

Sincerely,

Bruce B. Fairplay

Dataville Games Chairman
Dataville, USA

Reteaching Math: Data Analysis & Probability © 2008 by Bob Krech, Scholastic Teaching Resources

Name: _____ Date: _____

Dataville Annual Games Fair Attendance

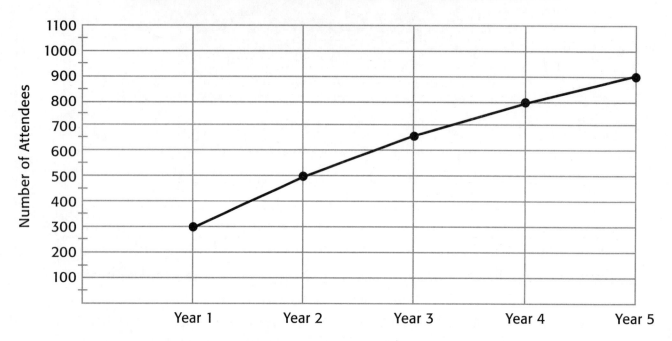

1. How many people came to the Games Fair in Year 1? _____

2. How many people came to the Games Fair in Year 3? _____

3. How many more people came in Year 3 than in Year 1? _____

4. Between which two consecutive years
   did the attendance increase the most? _____

5. By how many people did the attendance increase from Year 1 to Year 5? _____

6. Which one of the following statements is true? _____

   a. Attendance at the Games Fair has remained the same each year.

   b. Attendance has increased each year.

   c. Attendance decreased in Year 3.

   d. More people came in Year 3 than in Year 4.

Reteaching Math: Data Analysis & Probability © 2008 by Bob Krech, Scholastic Teaching Resources

Name: _____   Date: _____

Teams Participating Data/Line Graph

Number of Teams Participating in Sports Competition	
Year 1	3
Year 2	6
Year 3	5
Year 4	6
Year 5	8

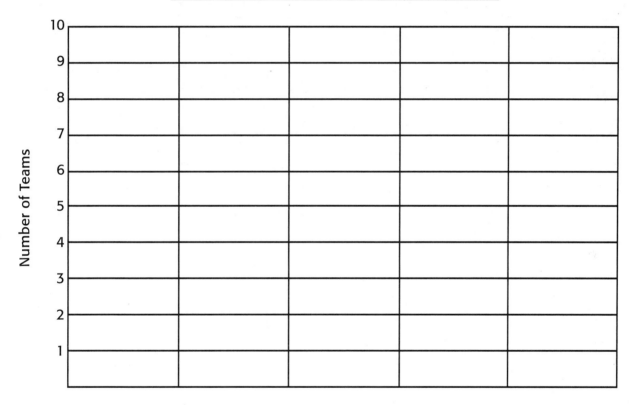

Year

Observations:

1. _____

2. _____

Reteaching Math: Data Analysis & Probability © 2008 by Bob Krech, Scholastic Teaching Resources

Name: _____   Date: _____

Pie Entries Data/Line Graph

Number of Entries in the Pie Contest	
Year 1	10 pies
Year 2	20 pies
Year 3	15 pies
Year 4	30 pies
Year 5	40 pies

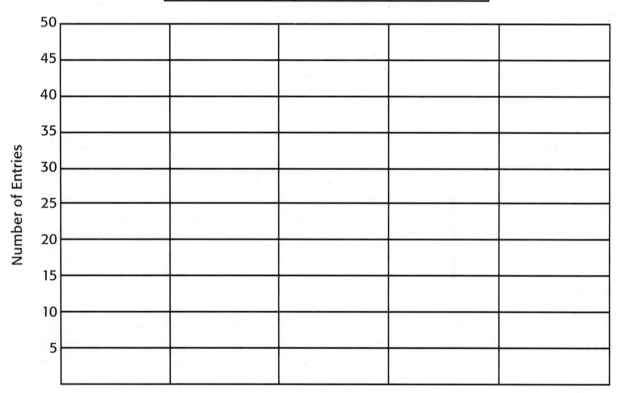

Observations:

1. _____

2. _____

Reteaching Math: Data Analysis & Probability © 2008 by Bob Krech, Scholastic Teaching Resources

Name: _____   Date: _____

Bowling Average Data/Line Graph

Bowling Average	
Year 1	130
Year 2	175
Year 3	155
Year 4	170
Year 5	160

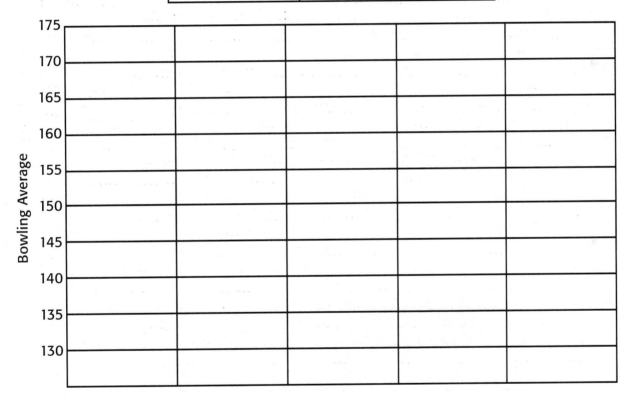

Observations:

1. _____

2. _____

Name: _____ Date: _____

WORD PROBLEM

Clifford Q. Gourd owns a Pick-Your-Own Pumpkin Farm. This line graph shows sales for the past 4 seasons. In which year did he sell the most pumpkins?

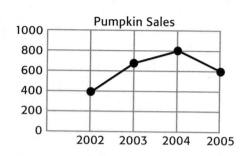

BASICS BOX

Line Graph

This type of graph shows change over time for data in a specific area. The numbers at the bottom of this graph show the years. The numbers on the left side show the number of pumpkins sold. A mark is made on the line where the year and the amount of pumpkins intersect. All marks are joined by a line, which makes the trend easy to see. On this line graph, you can see the highest point on the line is in the year 2004. Therefore, Mr. Gourd sold the most pumpkins in 2004.

PRACTICE

Zane has found a way to help save the planet and make a little money too. Zane collects empty bottles and cans and brings them to the recycling center each month. This line graph shows how many bottles and how many cans he collected each month this year.

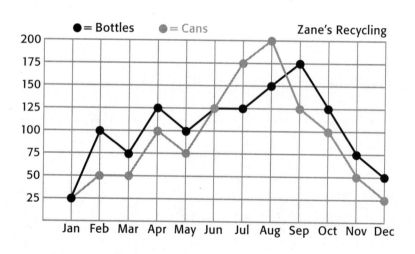

1. During which month did Zane bring the same amount of cans and bottles? _____

2. If Zane gets $0.02 for each can he brings to the recycling center, how much did he get for his cans in August? _____

JOURNAL

Make up your own line graph. Write two questions that could be answered from the data on your graph. Ask a friend to answer your questions.

Reteaching Math: Data Analysis & Probability © 2008 by Bob Krech, Scholastic Teaching Resources

Name: _____ Date: _____

Line Graphs

Absences for the School Year

1. How many children were absent in October? _____

2. Were more children absent in April or November?

    _____

3. During which months were the most children at school?

    _____

4. Which months had the most absences? _____

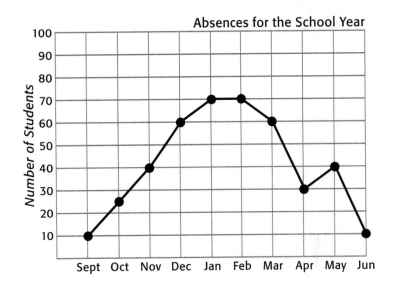

Cookie Sales in the Spring

5. Which type of cookie sold more in May? _____

6. During which month were the most peanut butter cookies sold?

    _____

7. How many more cases of peanut butter cookies than chocolate chip were sold in March?

    _____

8. How many cases of cookies were sold in June? _____

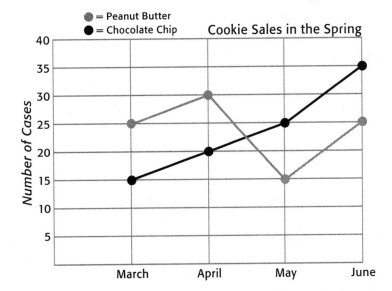

Reteaching Math: Data Analysis & Probability © 2008 by Bob Krech, Scholastic Teaching Resources

Dataville County Games

County of Dataville 13th Annual Games Fair

Dear Students,

Greetings from Dataville. As I am sure you know, participating in events such as the ones offered at our Games Fair certainly causes one to work up an appetite.

We have found that our Quick Stop Snack Shacks are a popular solution. These snack stops do not offer the menu selection of our regular food stand but instead offer snack/drink combinations for the low price of $1.50 per "combo." Each combo includes a drink and a snack. Below is a list of the drinks and snacks that are available.

Please use a tree diagram to determine how many different combos can be made. Then fill out the enclosed table listing all of the combo choices.

As always, your hard work is truly appreciated.

Sincerely,

Bruce B. Fairplay

Dataville Games Chairman
Dataville, USA

Drinks: Water, Fabulous 100% Fruit Juice (FFJ), Freshly Squeezed Lemonade

Snacks: Soft Pretzel, Popcorn, Pizza (slice), Nut Mix

Reteaching Math: Data Analysis & Probability © 2008 by Bob Krech, Scholastic Teaching Resources

Name: _____   Date: _____

Quick Stop Snack Shop
Combos Tree Diagram

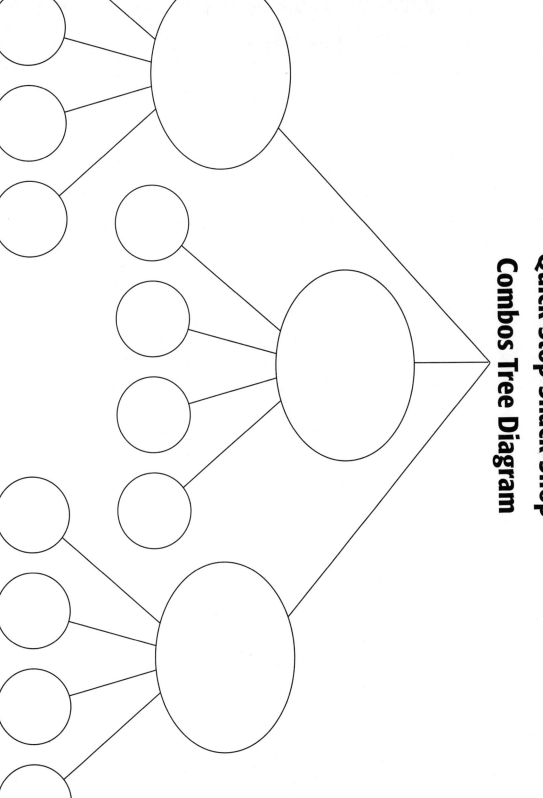

Reteaching Math: Data Analysis & Probability © 2008 by Bob Krech, Scholastic Teaching Resources

Name: _____ Date: _____

Quick Stop Snack Shop
Combos Table

Reteaching Math: Data Analysis & Probability © 2008 by Bob Krech, Scholastic Teaching Resources

Name: _____   Date: _____

Murray loves ice cream. Today he bought a half gallon of fudge ripple and a half gallon of cookie crunch. He also bought rainbow sprinkles, chocolate sprinkles, chocolate chips, and pineapple bits as toppings. How many different ice cream and topping combinations can he make?

BASICS BOX

A **tree diagram** is a good tool to use to organize data into all possible combinations. We know that each combination for Murray will have one ice cream flavor and one topping. Our tree diagram will start with two ice cream flavors. Next we add each topping to each flavor. This allows us to see how many combinations can be made. We follow the path of each line to see each possible combination.

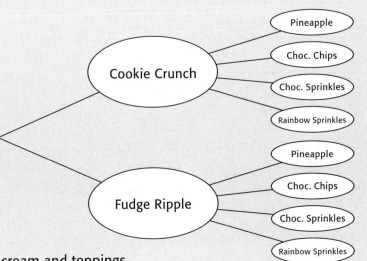

There are 8 possible combinations of ice cream and toppings.

PRACTICE

Dillon has a bag with the letters A, Q, B, and M inside and a bag with the numbers 4, 10, and 18 inside. Use a tree diagram to show all the possible combinations of these numbers and letters. How many different 1 letter/1 number combinations can he make?

JOURNAL

Explain why a tree diagram could be useful for a clothing company as they prepare a list of suggested outfits for their customers.

Name: _____ Date: _____

Tree Diagrams and Combinations

Draw tree diagrams and answer the questions.

1. On Fridays, the P.E. class and Art class join together for a Free Choice hour. Each child must pick one game and one craft to participate in. Here are this week's choices:

P. E.	Art
Volley ball	Painting
Relay races	Weaving
Freeze tag	Origami

How many choice combinations can you choose from? _____

2. Pizza by the Slice just opened a new shop. Mondays are free topping days. This Monday, the Special Board looked like this:

Pizza by the Slice
Choose whole wheat or regular crust
Choose thick or crispy crust
Choose 1 free topping! Pepperoni, Pineapple, or Broccoli

How many different combinations are possible? _____

Reteaching Math: Data Analysis & Probability © 2008 by Bob Krech, Scholastic Teaching Resources

County of Dataville 13th Annual Games Fair

Dear Students,

Greetings from the county of Dataville. I want to express my sincere thanks for all of your help in organizing the data from this year's Games Fair. It is because of students like you that we are able to record data in such an organized way in our Dataville Annual Games Fair Yearly Log and continue to make our Games Fair more exciting and enjoyable each year.

To entertain the participants and their families when they are not involved in one of the friendly competitions, we offer many games of chance in our Take a Chance Game Tent. Although we cannot offer you the actual games and prizes, we thought you might like to gain an understanding of the concept of probability behind these games of chance.

Enclosed you will find several activities and instruction cards. We hope you enjoy them as much as we have enjoyed working with you.

Sincerely,

Bruce B. Fairplay

Dataville Games Chairman
Dataville, USA

Activity Card #1: The Chances Are . . .

Materials for 3-5 players:

- paper bag with colored paper squares
- The Chances Are . . . Record Sheet
- pencil

Directions:

1. Take the cards out of the bag.
2. Fill in the top section of the recording sheet.
3. Put the cards back in the bag.
4. The first student picks a card without looking, records the result on the record sheet, and puts the card back in the bag.
5. Repeat Step 4 until each student in the group has had five "picks."
6. Discuss as a group the results that are on the record sheet:
7. Are these results what you thought would "probably" happen? Why or why not?

Activity Card #2: It's a Toss Up/Heads or Tails

Materials for 1 player:

- 1 coin
- Heads or Tails Record Sheet
- pencil

Directions:

1. Fill in the top section of the record sheet.
2. Toss the coin and mark the result on the record sheet using tally marks.
3. Repeat Step 2, either 25, 40, or 100 times (decide this ahead of time).
4. Compare your results with one or two other students.
5. Discuss your results with the class.

Activity Card #3: Very SPINteresting!

Materials for each student:

- 2 blank spinners
- crayons (blue, green, yellow, and red)
- 2 paper clips and 2 brass fasteners
- Very SPINteresting! Record Sheet
- pencil

Directions:

1. Color one of the spinners with one section of each of the four colors.
2. Color the second spinner with an uneven amount of one color. Choose two or three of the colors but do not make an even amount of each color on the sections.
3. Attach a paper clip with a brass fastener to the center of each spinner.
4. Give it a spin!
5. Using the Very SPINteresting! Record Sheet, do the activity first with your "fair" spinner and then with your "unfair" spinner.
6. Discuss your results with the class.

Reteaching Math: Data Analysis & Probability © 2008 by Bob Krech, Scholastic Teaching Resources

Name: _____   Date: _____

The Chances Are . . . Record Sheet

There are _____ colored squares in Bag # _____.

# of square	Color	Chance
		out of
		out of
		out of
		out of

"Pick" Results

Color	(Use tally marks to indicate each "pick.")

Our group noticed the following about our results:
_____
_____
_____

Reteaching Math: Data Analysis & Probability © 2008 by Bob Krech, Scholastic Teaching Resources

Name: _____   Date: _____

Probability Cartoons

Likely	Unlikely
_____ _____ _____	_____ _____ _____
Certain	**Impossible**
_____ _____ _____	_____ _____ _____

Reteaching Math: Data Analysis & Probability © 2008 by Bob Krech, Scholastic Teaching Resources

Name: _____ Date: _____

There are 12 marbles in a bag. 9 of the marbles are orange and 3 are green. Wayne reaches into the bag without looking and pulls out one marble. What probably happened?

BASICS BOX

When we talk about measuring the chances of something happening we are talking about **probability**, the mathematical study of chance. When Wayne reaches into the bag, he has a 9 out of 12 chance of picking an orange marble. The actual event or result when he picks something out is often called an **outcome**. He has a 3 out of 12 chance of picking a green marble so it is **likely** he will pick a green. Out of the 12 marbles, more of them are orange. So we can say that Wayne will probably pick out an orange marble. Since there are only three green marbles it is **not likely** that he will pick out a green marble.

= orange
= green

We can also say that it is **certain** that Wayne will pick either an orange marble or a green marble. Finally, we can say that it is **impossible** that Wayne will pick a red marble because there are no red marbles in the bag.

JOURNAL

Explain in words and pictures what a 7 out of 12 chance means.

PRACTICE

Myrna has a bag of shapes. If she reaches into the bag and pulls out one shape without looking what are the chances of each outcome listed. Choose likely, not likely, certain or impossible for each outcome.

1. Myrna pulls out a star.

2. Myrna pulls out a circle.

3. Myrna pulls out a fish or star.

Alvin, Andrew, Arthur, Alex, and Antonio, and you put your names in a hat. Mr. Arbuckle the accordion teacher will pick names out to decide the order of the performers in the concert.

4. On the first pick, what is the chance your name will be picked?

_____ out of _____

5. If Arthur's name is picked first, what is the chance your name will be picked next?

_____ out of _____

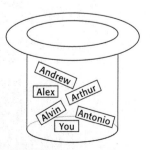

77

Name: _____   Date: _____

Understanding Probability

Write likely, not likely, certain, or impossible for each outcome. You reach in and randomly pull out . . .

a star

_____

a block

_____

a circle

_____

a triangle

_____

a moon

_____

Draw the objects in the box so that they have the following chance of being randomly selected. Then answer each question.

2 yellow squares

4 blue circles

4 orange triangles

1 yellow circle

2 blue triangles

2 orange squares

1. What is the chance that a circle will be selected? _____

2. What is the chance that a triangle will be selected? _____

3. What is the chance that a blue shape will be selected?

_____

Reteaching Math: Data Analysis & Probability © 2008 by Bob Krech, Scholastic Teaching Resources

Name: _____   Date: _____

Heads or Tails Record Sheet

I will toss the coin _____ times.

Possible Result	(Use tally marks to indicate each result.)

The coin landed on "heads" _____ times.

The coin landed on "tails" _____ times.

This is what I noticed about my results: _____

_____

Extra Practice

The party committee needs members to fill the following jobs

Job	Number of people
decorations	5
food	6
tickets	2
music	4

Total people needed _____

They put all of the positions into a hat so that each member of the committee could randomly choose a job. What is the chance that the first member will choose?

1. decorations _____ out of _____

2. food _____ out of _____

3. tickets _____ out of _____

4. music _____ out of _____

Name: _____   Date: _____

Very SPINteresting! Record Sheet

If you spin your "fair" spinner 40 times, what kind of results will probably occur and why?

_____

_____

1. Red has a _____ out of _____ chance.

2. Green has a _____ out of _____ chance.

3. Blue has a _____ out of _____ chance.

4. Yellow has a _____ out of _____ chance.

"Fair" Spinner Results

red	
blue	
green	
yellow	

Spin your "fair" spinner 40 times. Use tally marks to mark the results in the table above.

5. The spinner landed on red _____ times.

6. The spinner landed on green _____ times.

7. The spinner landed on blue _____ times.

8. The spinner landed on yellow _____ times.

"Unfair" Spinner Results

red	
blue	
green	
yellow	

Spin your "Unfair" spinner 40 times. Use tally marks to mark the results in the table above.

9. The spinner landed on red _____ times.

10. The spinner landed on green _____ times.

11. The spinner landed on blue _____ times.

12. The spinner landed on yellow _____ times.

13. Are these results what you thought would probably happen? _____ Why or why not? _____

_____

80

Reteaching Math: Data Analysis & Probability © 2008 by Bob Krech, Scholastic Teaching Resources

Name: _____ Date: _____

Make Your Own Spinners

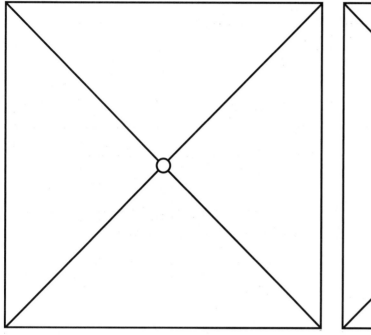 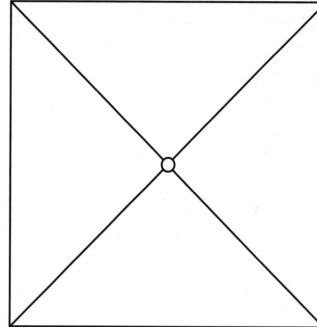

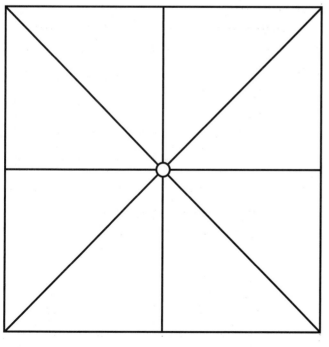 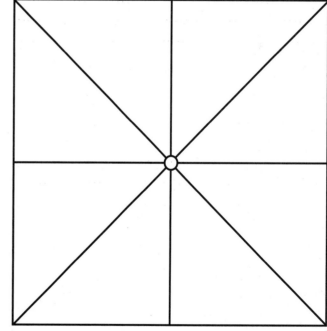

Name: _____ Date: _____

Lea spins a wheel that has four sections. Two of the sections are blue and two of the sections are yellow. If it lands on yellow, Lea wins. What are the chances of Lea winning?

BASICS BOX

Spinners are one way to generate a random outcome.

An **outcome** is what will happen as a result of spinning a spinner, or rolling dice, or spinning a wheel.

When we ask what the **chance** of something happening is, we are asking how likely it is that it will occur.

When Lea spins this wheel there are four possible outcomes. It could land on the first blue section, the second blue section, the first yellow section or the second yellow section. Lea wins if it lands on yellow so since there are four sections and two are yellow she has a $\frac{2}{4}$ chance of winning. We can also say there is a $\frac{1}{2}$ change or 50% chance.

PRACTICE

Four children are playing a game with this wheel. Next to their name below is the color they have chosen. Describe their chances of winning if we spin this wheel. Use a fraction and a word from the word box to answer.

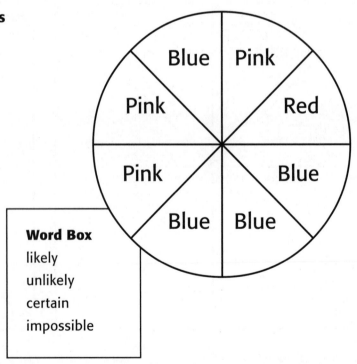

1. Terri – Red _____

   _____

2. Ron – Blue _____

   _____

3. Ted – Yellow _____

   _____

Word Box
likely
unlikely
certain
impossible

Reteaching Math: Data Analysis & Probability © 2008 by Bob Krech, Scholastic Teaching Resources

Name: _____   Date: _____

1. Preeti is tossing a coin. She has tossed it 15 times so far. Heads has come up 9 times and tails has come up 6 times. What are the chances that she will get heads on her next toss? Explain your answer.

    _____

    _____

2. Jan and Dean are spinning this wheel. If it lands on an odd number Dean wins. If it lands on an even number, Jan wins.

    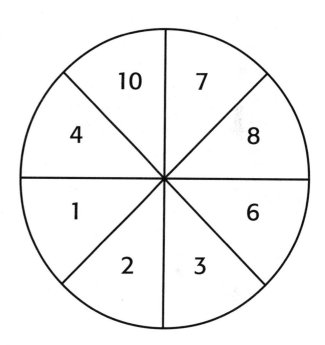

    a. What are the chances of Dean winning? _____

    b. What are the chances of Jan winning? _____

    c. How could this game be made more fair? _____

Draw a spinner that uses the numbers 3, 5, and 4. Make it a fair spinner. Explain why it is fair.

Name: _____   Date: _____

Probability With Coins and Spinners

Review

1. Tania has three coins; a penny, a nickel, and a dime. She is going to toss all of them at once and record the outcomes. Draw a table that shows all the possible outcomes Tania could get.

2. If you were playing a game with this spinner, would you rather have blue or red as your color? Why?

    _____

    _____

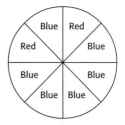

3. Looking at the spinner above, use a fraction to describe the chances of blue as an outcome. _____

4. Which of these spinners is fair? Explain your answer.

    _____

    _____

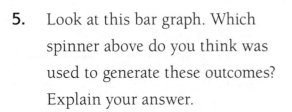

5. Look at this bar graph. Which spinner above do you think was used to generate these outcomes? Explain your answer.

    _____

    _____

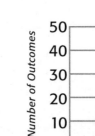

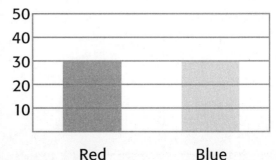

Reteaching Math: Data Analysis & Probability © 2008 by Bob Krech, Scholastic Teaching Resources

County of Dataville 13th Annual Games Fair

Dear Students,

We've been having a very smooth fair except for one problem in the Dueling Dice game. In this game the players reach into a bucket and pull out a ping-pong ball. Each ball is marked with a number. There are 11 numbers from 2 through 12. Once players have selected their number they line up to take turns rolling a pair of giant foam dice. Players keep rolling the dice until their number comes up ten times. The first player to do this wins.

Sounds like it's fun and fair, right? Well, we've been having a lot of complaints that the game isn't fair. I've included some testing materials here for you to help us research whether the game is fair or not and any recommendations you may have for us on how to make it fair. Thanks as always for your help.

Sincerely,

Bruce B. Fairplay

Dataville Games Chairman
Dataville, USA

Name: _____ Date: _____

 # Dice Roll Record Sheet

Sum	Tallies	Total
2		
3		
4		
5		
6		
7		
8		
9		
10		
11		
12		

What sum came up the most? _____ Why? _____

Reteaching Math: Data Analysis & Probability © 2008 by Bob Krech, Scholastic Teaching Resources

Dataville
County Games

County of Dataville 13th Annual Games Fair

Dear Students,

   We are considering adding a new game to next year's line up of games. This one is called Pick and Place. Using a deck of number cards (also known as digit cards) you play against a partner picking cards from the deck and placing them on a Pick and Place Board to try to create the largest possible four digit odd number. There are two of each number in the deck from 0 – 9.

   There is definitely some use of strategy and probability here, but I'm not sure how, what do you think? I hope you enjoy it. Thanks as always for your help.

Sincerely,

Bruce B. Fairplay

Dataville Games Chairman
Dataville, USA

Name: _____   Date: _____

Pick and Place Record Sheet

Place your digit cards face down and mix them up. Pick a card. Turn it over and place it on the place value board. Take turns picking numbers and placing them on your individual boards. Whoever gets the highest number wins. Record the numbers and words.

Bonus Win
Whoever gets the highest number overall by the end of the class is the bonus winner.

My numbers

number	word
725	Seven-hundred twenty-five

My partner's numbers

number	word
301	three hundred one

Reteaching Math: Data Analysis & Probability © 2008 by Bob Krech, Scholastic Teaching Resources

Name: _____   Date: _____

Pick and Place Board

Thousands	Hundreds	Tens	Ones
Thousands	Hundreds	Tens	Ones

Name: _____   Date: _____

Digit Cards

0	1	2	3	4	5
6	7	8	9	0	1
2	3	4	5	6	7
8	9	0	1	2	3
4	5	6	7	8	9

Reteaching Math: Data Analysis & Probability © 2008 by Bob Krech, Scholastic Teaching Resources

Name: _____   Date: _____

WORD PROBLEM

Pablo has six cards face down in front of him. There is a 1, 2, 3, 4, 5, and 7.
What is the probability that he will pick an odd number?

BASICS BOX

There are six possible outcomes for Pablo because there are six different cards.
Four of the possible outcomes are odd (1, 3, 5, and 7) while two of the possible
outcomes are even (2 and 4). The probability he will get an odd number is
good or likely. We could use a fraction to show that he has a $\frac{4}{6}$ chance or $\frac{2}{3}$
chance, which is a good likelihood of something happening.

PRACTICE

1. Jen rolls a pair of dice three times. She gets a sum of eleven, a sum of six, and a sum of
   seven. She predicts that these will be the numbers that come up the most even is she
   rolls the dice a hundred times. Do you agree? Why or why not?

   _____

   _____

2. If you roll a die, what are the chances that an odd number will come up? Explain.

   _____

   _____

3. Taquan is playing Pick and Place. He needs an 8 or 9 to win. The cards left in the deck
   are 7, 7, 3, 6, 8, 4, 2, and 9. What are his chances of winning if he has once pick left?
   Use a fraction and words to explain. _____

   _____

4. Madison can win a Pick and Place game with Leonard if she picks an odd number.
   When the game started there were 10 odd numbers in the deck. The cards left now are
   0, 0, 7, and 6. What are the chances of Madison winning? Use a fraction and words to
   explain. _____

   _____

JOURNAL

Why are dice and number cards good materials to use in games?

Name: _____ Date: _____

Probability With and Dice and Number Cards

Review

1. When you roll a pair of dice, what sum is most likely to come up the most? Why?

    _____

    _____

2. Tania is picking number cards from a deck. She needs an odd number to win. The cards that are left are 1, 0, 3, 9, 6, 5, and 1. What are her chances of winning?

    _____

    _____

3. Tyler is rolling dice. He says there are five ways to make a sum of 10 when rolling. He says you could get a 5 + 5, 6 + 4, 4 + 6, 7 + 3, or 3 + 7. Is he right? Why or why not?

    _____

    _____

4. Luther is playing a game with number cards. He picks four cards at a time and makes as many numbers as he can. If he picks a 4, 7, 3, and 2, what are all the two-digit numbers he can make?

    _____

    _____

5. When you are rolling dice what are the hardest sums to get? Why?

    _____

    _____

Reteaching Math: Data Analysis & Probability © 2008 by Bob Krech, Scholastic Teaching Resources

Practice Page #1 (p. 29)

1. goldfish
2. 107
3. goldfish, swordtail fish, angel fish, and zebra fish; These were the top four selling types of fish.

Journal: Wording of answers can vary but should show understanding that data is collected information, a survey is a method of collecting data and to analyze is to understand the data.

Review Page #1 (p. 30)

1. 94
2. return visitors
3. floor hockey
4. 15
5. Humor
6. Rita, Matt, and Jasmine
7. Mysteries
8. Rita, Matt, and Jasmine

Pictograph (p. 33)

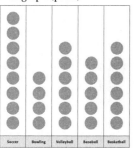

Bar Graph (p. 35)

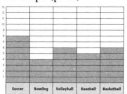

1. soccer
2. basketball
3. 2
4. bowling
5. 4
6. volleyball and basketball

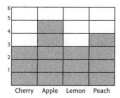

Practice Page #2 (p. 36)

1. 4   3. apple
2. 12   4. 15

Practice Page #2 (continued) (p. 37)

1. bike hike
2. 55
3. 3
4. the bar graph; Answers can vary but should show an understanding that the bar graph includes information about boys, girls, and totals but the pictograph only shows totals.

Journal: Answers can vary but should show an understanding that it is helpful to have a picture represent more than one thing and the scale count by larger numbers than 1 when there is a lot of data.

Review Page #2 (p. 38)

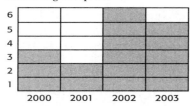

1. 8   4. Saturday
2. 3
3. 8-year-olds
4. Saturday
5. Saturday, Sunday, and Wednesday
6. weekdays

Bowling Competition Results Analysis (p. 41)

	Brook Point	Marshtown	Stream Valley	Fountain Woods
How many bowlers were on the team?	7	7	7	7
How many bowlers scored 150 or higher?	0	5	7	7
What was the lowest score?	140	145	150	156
What was the highest score?	149	154	156	162
Find the range for each team.	9	9	6	6

Combined Bowling Results (p. 42)

1. 28   4. 140
2. 19   5. range = 22 (162 – 140)
3. 162   6. Answers will vary.

Practice Page #3 (p. 43)

Practice: Answers will vary.

Journal: Answers will vary but should show an understanding that both display data, the horizontal line of the line plot is similar to the marking on the bar graph which can be along the bottom or to the left side of the bar graph, the line plot uses individual marks and the bar graph uses a series of connected boxes forming a bar.

Review Page #3 (p. 44)

1. 27 children
2. 49 cans
3. 45 cans
4. 22 children
5. range = 24

Line Plot:

6. 78
7. 88
8. 9
9. range = 20

History of High and Low Bowling Scores (p. 45)

1. Range = 11
2. Mean = 271
3. Median = 270.5
4. Mode = 269
5. Range = 8
6. Mean = 118
7. Median = 118
8. Mode = 118

Practice Page #4 (p. 46)

1. Mean = 34, Median = 28, Mode = 21, Range = 42
2. Mean = 34, Median = 36, Mode = 36, Range = 37

Journal: Answers will vary.

Review Page #4 (p. 47)

1. 4
2. 5
3. 5
4. 37
5. 123
6. 13
7. 8
8. 24
9. 67
10. Mean = 32, Mode = 24, Median = 32 Range = 22

Letter #5/Two-Circle Venn Diagram (pp. 48 and 49)

1.

2.
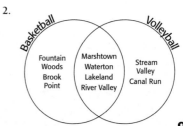

3.

4.

5.

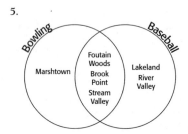

6.

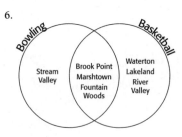

Letter #5/Three-Circle Venn Diagram (pp. 48 and 50)

1.

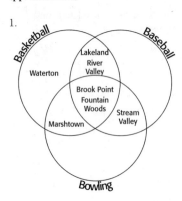

2.

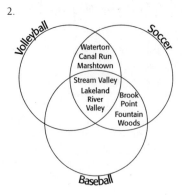

3.

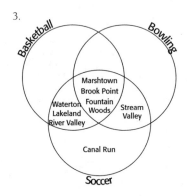

Practice Page #5 (p. 51)

1. 9
2. 12
3. 4
Journal:

Review Page #5 (p. 52)

1. 9
2. Frances, Ed, Ty, Wayne
3. 2
4. Debbie, Lisa, and Marie
5. 10
6. 8
7. 2
8. Dina

Dataville 13th Annual Pie Contest (p. 54)

1. 40
2. peach pie
3. 5
4. rhubarb and mixed fruit
5. apple and mixed fruit
6. 9
7. 30

8. 10, 40
9. 15, 40
10. 4, 40
11. 6, 40
12. 5, 40

Practice Page #6 (p. 55)

1. 24
2. 9
3. props
4. 12
5. backstage activities

Practice Page #6 (continued) (p. 56)

1. Language Arts
2. 60 minutes
3. Spanish
4. Science or Social Studies
5. 360
Journal: Answers may vary but should show an understanding that the pieces of the pie chart all come together to create the whole thing.

Review Page #6 (p. 57)
Chart: Vanessa's Allowance

1. 100
2. 13
3. food
4. $50.00
5. second grade
6. kindergarten

Practice Page #7 (p. 59)

1. Dobermans: 5/50 or 1/10
2. Soccer drills: 40/90 or 4/9
Journal: Answers will vary.

Review Page #7 (p. 60)

1. 5/20 or 1/4
2. 9/24 or 3/8
3. 5/19
4. 22/37
5. 6/21 or 2/7
6. 7/49 or 1/7
7.

8.

9.

Dataville Annual Games Fair Attendance (p. 62)
1. 300
2. 650
3. 350
4. years 1 and 2
5. 600
6. b

Teams Participating (p. 63)

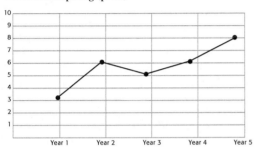

Pie Entries (p. 64)

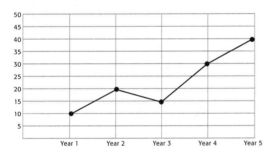

Bowling Average (p. 65)

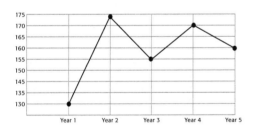

Practice Page #8 (p. 66)
1. June
2. $3.00
Journal: Answers will vary.

Review Page #8 (p. 67)
1. 25
2. November
3. September and June
4. January and February
5. Chocolate Chip
6. April
7. 10
8. 60

Quick Stop Snack Shop Combos Tree Diagram (p. 69)

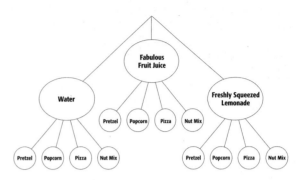

Quick Stop Snack Shop Combos Table (p. 70)
Water and Pretzel
Water and Popcorn
Water and Pizza
Water and Nut Mix
Fabulous Fruit Juice and Pretzel
Fabulous Fruit Juice and Popcorn
Fabulous Fruit Juice and Pizza
Fabulous Fruit Juice and Nut Mix
Freshly Squeezed Lemonade and Pretzel
Freshly Squeezed Lemonade and Popcorn
Freshly Squeezed Lemonade and Pizza
Freshly Squeezed Lemonade and Nut Mix

Practice Page #9 (p. 71)
12 possible combinations

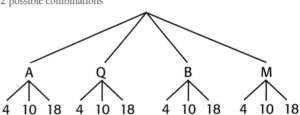

Review Page #9 (p. 72)
1. 9 possible combinations

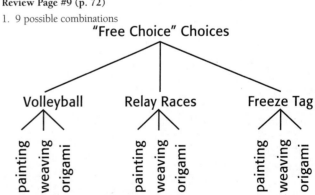

2. 12 possible combinations

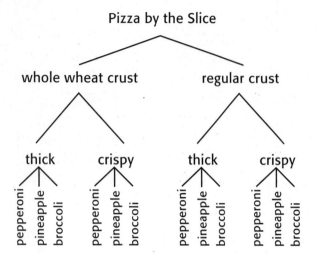

Pizza by the Slice

whole wheat crust — regular crust

thick — crispy — thick — crispy

pepperoni / pineapple / broccoli (under each: thick and crispy, whole wheat and regular)

Practice Page #10 (p. 77)
1. Likely
2. Impossible
3. Certain
4. 1 out of 6
5. 1 out of 5
Journal: Answers will vary.

Review Page #10 (p. 78)
Shapes: certain, impossible, not likely, likely, likely
Colors/Shapes:

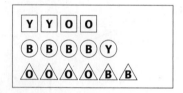

Y Y O O
B B B B Y
O O O O B B

1. 5 out of 15
2. 6 out of 15
3. 6 out of 15

Heads or Tails Record Sheet (p. 79)
Heads or Tails: Answer will vary.
Party Committee: 17 people
1. 5 out of 17
2. 6 out of 17
3. 2 out of 17
4. 4 out of 17

Practice Page #11/#12 (p. 82)
1. 1/8, unlikely
2. 4/8, likely
3. 0/8, impossible

Practice Page #11/#12 (continued) (p. 83)
1. Preeti has a 1 out of 2 or a 50% chance on getting heads. Each time she tosses the coin, she has the same possibility of getting heads.
2a. 3 out of 8 chance
2b. 5 out of 8 chance
2c. This game could be made more fair by having the same amount of odd and even numbers.
Journal: Answers may vary but each spinner must have all three numbers the same amount of times.

Review Page #11/#12 (p. 84)
1. 8 possible combinations
2. Answers may vary but the most common answer will probably be blue because there is a 6 out of 8 chance of landing on blue and only a 2 out of 8 chance of landing on red.
3. 6/8 or 3/4
4. The second one because each color has the same amount of chances: 2 out of 4 or 2/4 or 1/2 or 50%. In the first spinner the red had a 2/3 chance and the blue has a 1/3 chance.
5. The second one because the results are equal. If the first one was used, there would more likely be more red results.

Penny	Nickel	Dime
H	H	H
H	H	T
H	T	H
H	T	T
T	T	T
T	T	H
T	H	H
T	H	T

Practice Page #13/#14 (p. 91)
1. Answers will vary but should show understanding that there are 36 possible combinations and 11 possible sums. The sum of 11 only has a 2 out of 36 chance of being rolled. The sum of 6 has 5 possible combinations and the sum of 7 has 6 possible combinations. It is more likely that the sum of 7 or 6 will be rolled than the sum of 11. The sums of 4, 5, 8, 9, 10 are also more likely than the sum of 11.
2. There is a 3/6 or 1/2 or 50% chance that an odd number will come up because 3 of the 6 numbers on a die are odd.
3. Taquan has a 2/8 or 1/4 chance of winning. There are 8 cards left and 2 of those 8 will result in a win. It is unlikely that he will win.
4. Madison has a 1/4 chance of winning because only 1 of the 4 cards left is odd. It is unlikely that she will win.
Journal: Answers will vary but may include that with both dice and number cards, each result has a fair chance of occurring.

Review Page #13/#14 (p. 92)
1. Seven is most likely to come up because 7 has the highest number of possible combinations.
2. Tania has a 5/7 chance of winning. It is likely that she will win.
3. No, There are three ways; a die only goes up to 6.
4. 47, 43, 42, 74, 73, 72, 34, 37, 32, 24, 27, 23
5. 2 and 12 are the hardest sums to get because there is only one combination for each of them.